Contested Territories and International Law

This book considers the possibilities for resolution of the Nagorno-Karabakh Conflict in the context of comparative international law. The armed conflict between Armenia and Azerbaijan over the territory of the Nagorno-Karabakh has been on the peace and security agenda since the dissolution of the Soviet Union. This volume draws parallels with a similar situation between Sweden and Finland over sovereignty of the Aland Islands in the early 20th century. Resolved in 1921, it is argued that this represents a model autonomy solution for territorial conflicts that include questions of territorial integrity, self-determination and minority rights. The book compares both conflict situations from the international law perspective, finding both commonalities and dissimilarities. It advances the application of the solution found in the Aland Islands precedent as a model for the resolution of the Nagorno-Karabakh Conflict, and provides appropriate recommendations for its implementation.

The book will be of interest to academics, researchers and policy-makers in the areas of international law and security, conflict resolution and international relations.

Kamal Makili-Aliyev is a Senior Lecturer at Malmö University, Sweden, researcher at the Faculty of Law of Lund University and at the Raoul Wallenberg Institute of Human Rights and Humanitarian Law. He previously worked in the fields of international law and international relations (specializing in the international security, defense and conflict) as the Senior Research Fellow at the Center for Strategic Studies (SAM) and as the Senior Legal Officer in the Ministry of Defense of Azerbaijan. Kamal Makili-Aliyev has also served as a Vice-Rector of Lomonosov Moscow State University Baku Branch and Senior Legal Advisor at the Constitutional Court of Azerbaijan. He is a Fellow of National Security Institute in Amherst, MA (U.S.).

Contested Territories and International Law

A Comparative Study of the Nagorno-Karabakh Conflict and the Aland Islands Precedent

Kamal Makili-Aliyev

Routledge
Taylor & Francis Group
LONDON AND NEW YORK

First published 2020
by Routledge
2 Park Square, Milton Park, Abingdon, Oxon OX14 4RN

and by Routledge
52 Vanderbilt Avenue, New York, NY 10017

Routledge is an imprint of the Taylor & Francis Group, an informa business

British Library Cataloguing-in-Publication Data
A catalogue record for this book is available from the British Library

Library of Congress Cataloging-in-Publication Data
Names: Makili-Aliyev, Kamal, 1985-author.
Title: Contested territories and international law: a comparative study of the Nagorno-Karabakh conflict and the Aland Islands precedent/Kamal Makili-Aliyev.
Description: Abingdon, Oxon; New York, NY: Routledge, 2019. | Includes bibliographical references and index.
Identifiers: LCCN 2019033606 (print) | LCCN 2019033607 (ebook) | ISBN 9780367373825 (hardback) | ISBN 9780429353437 (ebook)
Subjects: LCSH: Nagorno-Karabakh (Azerbaijan)–International status. | Nagorno-Karabakh Conflict, 1988-1994. | Åland question. | International law.
Classification: LCC KZ4314.M34 2019 (print) | LCC KZ4314 (ebook) | DDC 947.54086–dc23
LC record available at https://lccn.loc.gov/2019033606
LC ebook record available at https://lccn.loc.gov/2019033607

ISBN: 978-0-367-37382-5 (hbk)
ISBN: 978-0-367-40520-5 (pbk)
ISBN: 978-0-429-35343-7 (ebk)

DOI: 10.4324/9780429353437

Typeset in Galliard
by Deanta Global Publishing Services, Chennai, India

Dedicated to my wife Irina Galaeva. Thank you for all your patience and support.

Contents

Acknowledgments

The author would like to acknowledge and sincerely and deeply thank the Faculty of Law of Lund University who have hosted the research presented in this book.

The author would also like to specially thank and extend deep appreciation to Karol Nowak without whose mentorship and support this book would not be possible.

Special thanks to the Åland Islands Peace Institute and its director, Sia Spiliopoulou Åkermark, for their engagement and open discussions that helped a lot.

Introduction

The war in the region of South Caucasus is ongoing. The region itself is home not only to the three post-Soviet republics of Armenia, Azerbaijan and Georgia that are surrounded by the much bigger states of Iran, Russia and Turkey, but also to three out of five armed conflicts plaguing the post-Soviet space. All of these ongoing conflicts are products of the fall of the Soviet Union. Except for the conflict in the Eastern Ukraine that started in 2014, all other conflicts began with the dissolution of the USSR. Moldova is engaged in a conflict with its province of Transnistria, where there is a presence of Russian armed forces, and Georgia is in a conflict with its provinces of South Ossetia and Abkhazia. More recently (since 2008) Georgia is, technically, in conflict with Russia itself over the aforementioned territories.

Then, there is the Nagorno-Karabakh Conflict. What makes it somewhat unique and different from the other conflicts in the post-Soviet space is that there is no visible Russian presence there (at least officially and on the ground). This international armed conflict has been ongoing since the dissolution of the USSR (and with no resolution in sight) between Armenia and Azerbaijan over the territory of Nagorno-Karabakh, an enclave with a predominantly Armenian population landlocked in the territory of Azerbaijan. At least that is the status officially. It so happens that the South Caucasus as a region is of great geopolitical interest to regional players such as Iran, Russia and Turkey and even extra-regional players such as the EU, Israel and the U.S. Due to that fact, the "war" that rages in the South Caucasus is not only limited to the conflicts of Armenia, Azerbaijan and Georgia, but it also covers the battle of interests that all of the interested parties are waging in the region. This makes the Nagorno-Karabakh Conflict a very special case not only from the point of view of international law and conflict studies but also in terms of geopolitics and international relations. Nonetheless, while this study will attempt to tackle the question of the resolution of the Nagorno-Karabakh Conflict, it will try to distance itself from the political and the historical discourses and concentrate on the legal analysis and international law as much as possible. Political and historical discourses will be represented here only when necessary to lay the groundwork for the comprehensive international legal analysis.

It can be argued that most recent history has seen examples indicating that normative considerations for conflict resolution by themselves may fail to deliver the actual resolution of the conflicts. For example, in the case of Catalonia, the occupation of Crimea or even in the political recognition of occupied Golan Heights by the U.S. president, normative considerations and international law were cast aside in favor of political (non-normative) considerations. In this line of argument, the same can be applied to the Nagorno-Karabakh Conflict. The political considerations will always be important in conflict resolution and compete with international law. However, it is the normative basis for conflict resolution that allows for peaceful and civil resolution of any conflict and not political interests and considerations. While international law is heavily dependent on the will of the states, it binds them nonetheless with the particular code of conduct that should be applied to conflict situations, and thus, thoroughly studied. Here, then, the question arises: why is an international legal analysis so important and necessary in this particular case?

First, international law and its application to the Nagorno-Karabakh Conflict is gravely understudied and barely visible in international legal doctrine and discourse. This can be ameliorated by the comprehensive research on public international law in the Nagorno-Karabakh Conflict. Second, the current narrative in the process of the resolution of the Nagorno-Karabakh Conflict is very far away from the international law that is supposed to be the instrument for the resolution of any and all armed conflicts. Thus, this book will attempt to provide an answer to the question of how to return the narrative of the Nagorno-Karabakh Conflict back into the sphere of international law. It will also aim to contribute to the understanding of the legal nature of the conflict and serve as an academic base for solving this issue peacefully, without resort to use of force (even in self-defense), through international legal means available and provide the guidelines for governments concerned on how to approach the conflict from the viewpoint of international law.

While the Nagorno-Karabakh Conflict and its resolution are the main focus of this book, it is structured as a comparative international legal analysis. This is due to the fact that one of the main dilemmas of the Nagorno-Karabakh Conflict is the completely opposite points of view of the parties to the conflict about its resolution. While Armenia sees the resolution of the conflict in the territory of the Nagorno-Karabakh becoming an independent state or being incorporated into the territory of Armenia, Azerbaijan does not see the territory of Nagorno-Karabakh outside the boundaries of its own territorial integrity. Armenia, in turn, is explaining its position with the safety, security and self-determination of the Armenian population in the Nagorno-Karabakh. It so happens that it is not the first time in the history of mankind that such questions have been a matter of dispute between two or more states.

One such case is the Aland Islands. In the beginning of the XX century, these islands were a matter of territorial dispute between Sweden and Finland. After the independence of Finland from Imperial Russia, the Aland Islands, with a predominantly Swedish and Swedish-speaking population, were inclined to be returned to the kin-state; however, Finland did not agree to that. The conflict found its resolution through the peaceful mediation of the League of Nations and under the provisions of the international law at that time. The Aland Islands became an autonomous region in Finland with a very high level of self-governance. Until today, the Aland Islands precedent is an example of one of the most successful conflict resolution cases based on autonomy. The question then arises: why cannot the same be an example for the resolution of the Nagorno-Karabakh Conflict?

To answer this question, the book will compare the cases of the Aland Islands and Nagorno-Karabakh from the perspective of international law with the purpose of finding an applicable solution to the latter conflict through best practices that can be drawn from the success of the former precedent. Structured in four parts, the book provides a comprehensive legal analysis of each case in a separate chapter and then dedicates another chapter to the comparison of the Aland Islands precedent and the Nagorno-Karabakh Conflict under the international law. The last part of the book is dedicated to the proposed resolution of the Nagorno-Karabakh Conflict based on the Aland Islands precedent. In addition, it provides a specific set of recommendations in the form of principles to be applied for the peaceful resolution of the conflict under international law.

1 Nagorno-Karabakh Conflict in international law

The Nagorno-Karabakh Conflict is one of the gravest conflicts in the modern history of mankind. This conflict still poses a considerable threat to international peace and security as well as to the welfare of the states in the region of the South Caucasus. This chapter provides a comprehensive overview of the questions this conflict raises in regard to international law. It will make clear arguments on what international law actually says in regard to the conflict's two main sets of questions. The first set of questions are in connection with the role of Armenia in the conflict. Is Armenia just a kin-state trying to help in a just cause? Or is it an occupier of parts of the sovereign territory of its neighbor? The second set of questions are those that are concerned with the status and legitimacy of the separatist entity created in Nagorno-Karabakh, the so-called "Nagorno-Karabakh Republic" (hereinafter the "NKR").

Despite the fact that the arguments of the author can be summed up in approximately 800 words of an opinion article[1] that argues that the Nagorno-Karabakh territory is occupied and "NKR" and its self-determination claims have no legal grounds or support in international law, this book requires more than a quick summary. Hence, a thorough legal analysis of public international law will be provided to explain this chapter's claims. The analysis, however, will exclude discussions on international human rights law, international humanitarian law and international criminal law – for two main reasons. First, these questions were raised and discussed by the author in his previous research.[2] Second, for the purposes of this book, discussion of humanitarian aspects, justice and human rights is

1 Kamal Makili-Aliyev, *Nagorno-Karabakh Isn't Disputed Territory — It's Occupied – The National Interest (U.S.)*, May 2016, http://bit.ly/2eQt8v9

2 Kamal Makili-Aliyev, *Nagorno-Karabakh Conflict in International Legal Documents and International Law*, Baku: SAM, 2013, http://bit.ly/31qCYY4, pp. 24–73.

DOI: 10.4324/9780429353437-1

unnecessary, due to the fact that it will compare the Nagorno-Karabakh Conflict to the precedent that mainly features fundamental concepts of international law such as sovereignty, territorial integrity, peaceful resolution of conflicts, etc., and has no particular humanitarian features to be used in such a comparison.

Thus, human rights in general and humanitarian aspects of the conflict as well as international criminal justice will be excluded from the overview of international law in the context of the Nagorno-Karabakh Conflict. On the other hand, such issues as the use of principles of territorial integrity and rights of peoples to self-determination, implementation of UN Security Council resolutions, right to self-defense of Azerbaijan, Montevideo Convention of 1933 and its applicability to "NKR", soviet legacy legislation, principle of *uti possidetis juris*, and others in regard to this Conflict will be discussed further in greater detail.

Enter the Conflict: a brief historical overview

Karabakh is a small mountainous land that lies in the wider region of South Caucasus that historically has been located in the nexus of three empires: Russian (today, Russian Federation), Persian (today, Islamic Republic of Iran) and Ottoman (today, Republic of Turkey). Today South Caucasus consists of three independent states of Armenia, Azerbaijan and Georgia, which regained their independence after the dissolution of the Soviet Union in 1991. Armenians and Azerbaijanis lived in Karabakh for centuries and both trace their ancestry to the Caucasian Albania. They have always been in the middle of the clash of the empires warring in South Caucasus throughout the centuries. Probably the biggest demographic shift that established the majority of the Armenian population in the highland part of the region called Nagorno-Karabakh was in the beginning of the XIX century after the wars between Russian and Persian empires. The Armenian population in this territory dramatically increased, while Azeris, Kurds and Lezgins were being driven out.[3]

The dispute over the territory of Nagorno-Karabakh first arose between Armenia and Azerbaijan when these countries had their first chance to become sovereign independent states in 1918 after the revolution in the Russian Empire. At the time, even Armenians living in Karabakh agreed

3 Svante E. Cornell, *The Nagorno-Karabakh Conflict*, Report no. 46, Department of East European Studies, Uppsala University, 1999, p. 4; Christopher Rossi, 'Nagorno-Karabakh and the Minsk Group: The Imperfect Appeal of Soft Law in an Overlapping Neighborhood', *Texas International Law Journal*, No. 52 (1), 2017, pp. 54–55.

that it should be a part of Azerbaijan, with territorial and cultural autonomy for its Armenian population.[4] Later, in 1920, the Paris Peace Conference recognized Karabakh as belonging to Azerbaijan.[5] Ironically, by 1921 all of the states of South Caucasus had lost their newly gained independence and were already under Soviet rule. That year Nagorno-Karabakh was confirmed as a part of Azerbaijan (Azerbaijan Soviet Socialist Republic at that time) with the creation of regional autonomy there in order to maintain the economic ties between Nagorno-Karabakh (mountainous part) and lower Karabakh.[6] Interestingly, international historian Arsene Saparov states that:

> It has become almost cliché to blame the creation of the ethnic Armenian autonomy within Azerbaijan on Stalin, who by doing this created leverage against both republics. It seems the absence of any Russian-language works on the subject is partially responsible for such lack of historical insight.[7]

Indeed, the Armenian discourse on the Nagorno-Karabakh Conflict has adopted this narrative and used it in an attempt to justify the necessity of correcting what is perceived as a historical injustice perpetrated by Stalin. However, it is at the very least questionable due to the fact that one of the supporters of this decision in 1921 was an Armenian communist, Nazaretian.[8] Moreover, Saparov himself in his very detailed study of the subject comes to the conclusion that for Soviets, the "genuine desire to solve . . . conflicts was constrained by the need to accommodate the national interests of Caucasian republics. In the case of Karabakh, the granting of an autonomous status was a compromise solution".[9] Thus, the Soviets' decision to leave Karabakh in Azerbaijan was a rational decision rather than one based on ephemeral ethno-national policies. While in some other situations it may have been true that leverage policies were implemented by Stalin's regime, in the case of Nagorno-Karabakh this was not what happened.

4 Audrey L. Altstadt, *The Azerbaijani Turks: Power and Identity Under Russian Rule*, Stanford, CA: Hoover Institution, Press, 1992, p. 102.

5 Tim Potier, *Conflict in Nagorno-Karabakh, Abkhazia and South Ossetia. A Legal Appraisal*, The Hague: Kluwer Law International, 2001, p. 2.

6 Christopher Zurcher, *Post-Soviet Wars, Rebellion, Ethnic Conflict, and Nationhood in the Caucasus*, New York: New York University Press, 2007, p. 154.

7 Arsène Saparov, 'Why Autonomy? The Making of Nagorno-Karabakh Autonomous Region 1918–1925', *Europe-Asia Studies*, Volume 64, March 2012, p. 282.

8 Potier, *supra* note 5, p. 4.

9 Saparov, *supra* note 7, p. 321.

In light of the aforementioned arguments, several clarifications should be made. Despite the fact that a dispute around Nagorno-Karabakh was already present at the beginning of the XX century, it cannot be seen as the starting point for the Nagorno-Karabakh Conflict itself. The Soviet Union was created and existed for seven decades and has been recognized as a sovereign state that has made a tremendous impact on the modern world and the current international situation. Thus, the legality of this state cannot be questioned and is not considered in this work by the author. The illustration of the aforementioned dispute at the beginning of the XX century and its consequences are required for the understanding of the arguments in international law applicable to the Nagorno-Karabakh Conflict that will be provided further in this book.

With that said, the actual Nagorno-Karabakh Conflict began in 1988 when the Armenian population of Nagorno-Karabakh, with the support of the then Armenian Soviet Socialist Republic demanded secession of the territory of the Nagorno-Karabakh Autonomous Oblast' (hereinafter NKAO) from the territory of then Azerbaijan Soviet Socialist Republic and transfer of that territory to Armenia. In the period of 1988–1991, Azerbaijan and Armenian Soviet Socialist Republics and NKAO adopted a number of decisions that ranged from transfer of NKAO to the jurisdiction of Armenia to abolition of the NKAO autonomy by Azerbaijan, none of which have been accepted as legal and have been abolished by the central powers of Soviet Union in Moscow in 1991.[10] First clashes between Armenian and Azerbaijani forces began during the fall of 1991, even before the dissolution of the Soviet Union and on the background of a) the confusion in the Soviet army, b) actual loss of control of republican governments in the still Soviet Armenia and Azerbaijan over their armed units and c) common understanding that USSR is coming to an end.[11]

After the dissolution of the Soviet Union in late 1991, the Nagorno-Karabakh Conflict went into full-scale war between Armenia and Azerbaijan, which were newly independent and recognized *uti possidetis juris* in their territorial borders, just as they had existed in the former USSR. The result of the war was one of the bloodiest outcomes of all the conflicts in the post-Soviet era, with at least 25,000 lives lost. Moreover, the conflict left approximately one million Azerbaijani people internally displaced as refugees and around 20% of Azerbaijani territories occupied. A shaky cease-fire agreement has been maintained between the parties since

10 Potier, *supra* note 5, pp. 6–8.
11 Cornell, *supra* note 3, p. 25.

1994.[12] Not only Azerbaijan has suffered from conflict; the International Crisis Group estimates the number of displaced Armenians to be as high as 400,000.[13] The conflict continues at the time of writing of this book with low-intensity hostilities along the line of contact between armies of Armenia and Azerbaijan, with occasional flare-ups. The most intense such flare-up dates to April 2016 and was nicknamed by the international media and international researchers as a "Four-Day War".[14]

Role of Armenia in the Conflict: intervention of a concerned kin-state or clear and simple occupation?

The international community has condemned the occupation of Azerbaijani territories and the aggression of Armenia many times in multiple international legal instruments and called for and demanded the withdrawal of Armenian Armed Forces from the occupied Azerbaijani territories on several occasions to no avail. Most notable of these legal documents are United Nations (UN) Security Council resolutions 822, 853, 874 and 884 of 1993. Moreover, similar resolutions and declarations were adopted by the UN General Assembly, the European Parliament, the Parliamentary Assembly of the Council of Europe, the Organization of Islamic Cooperation and even NATO, which mentions in its declaration the unresolved conflicts in Nagorno-Karabakh as well as Georgia and Moldova in a long list of security challenges facing the West. It seems to single out territorial integrity of internationally recognized states as the guiding principle for their peaceful resolution. Moreover, that document makes no references to people's right to self-determination, which has been championed by the Armenian side.[15]

Despite all of the resolutions and declarations cited here, it is important for the purposes of this book and proper argumentation to set aside these

12 Kamer Kasim, 'The Nagorno-Karabakh Conflict: Regional Implications and the Peace Process', *Caucasus International*, Ankara: Moda Ofset Basim Yayin, Volume 2, No. 1, 2012, p. 94.

13 International Crisis Group, *Nagorno-Karabakh: Risking War*, Europe Report No. 187, I n.2, 2007.

14 Agha Bayramov, 'Silencing the Nagorno-Karabakh Conflict and Challenges of Four-Day War', *Security and Human Rights*, No. 27, 2016, p. 117.

15 UN General Assembly, *Resolution 62/243*; *PACE Resolution 1416* (2005) 'The conflict over the Nagorno-Karabakh Region Dealt with by the OSCE Minsk Conference'; *European Parliament resolution of 20 May 2010 on the need for an EU strategy for the South Caucasus* (2009/2216(INI)), paras. 8, 11, 41; *OIC Resolution no. 10/11-P(IS) on the Aggression of the Republic of Armenia against the Republic of Azerbaijan*; NATO, *Chicago Summit Declaration*, para. 47.

documents of international bodies for the moment and examine the international law itself. Let us suppose that international organizations have been wrong in their assessments of the situation in Nagorno-Karabakh, that all of their decisions and resolutions have political rather than legal motivation and that Armenia is not an aggressor and occupant of a neighboring state's territories in the Nagorno-Karabakh Conflict and is simply a kin-state trying to aid its national minority in a difficult situation. In other words, let us begin with *a contrario* reasoning.

The first sign that puts the aforementioned argument under reasonable doubt lies in the origins of the inception of the conflict in 1988. Back then, it was quite obvious that Nagorno-Karabakh Armenians had a clear, single-minded focus on their goal of unification with Armenia and that the Armenian government was ready to provide all the necessary support for this goal to be realized in practice and supported the bid of NKAO openly.[16] Despite the initial divisions in views between the Nagorno-Karabakh Armenians and the Armenians in Yerevan, on the background of rising violence between Armenians and Azerbaijanis, those groups have become united on the issue of the conflict very rapidly. The Armenian government in Yerevan was able to use the rise of nationalism among Armenians from both groups and inter-ethnic violence quite effectively to gain more power and reach its own goals.[17] It is thus clear that from the start the involvement of Armenia in the conflict was openly more than just actions of a concerned kin-state.

Furthermore, by the personal accounts of former defense minister of Armenia, Vazgen Manukian, the Karabakh Armenians and the Armenian Army were united in military actions during the war in 1991–1994.[18] That Armenian Armed Forces have been actively participating in the capture and occupation of the former NKAO and seven adjacent regions of Azerbaijan was recorded as early as 1994 by the NGO Human Rights Watch. Despite that fact, the Armenian military command denied military involvement, stating that no troops under their command and jurisdiction have been fighting in Karabakh and that no one that is serving in the Armenian Armed Forces can become a volunteer for Karabakh Armenians. Even Alexander Arzoumanian, the UN Ambassador of Armenia at the time, has denied the involvement of the Armenian Armed Forces, stating that there are no

16 *See*, Potier, *supra* note 5, pp. 6–7.

17 Nina Caspersen, 'Between Puppets and Independent Actors: Kin-state Involvement in the Conflicts in Bosnia, Croatia and Nagorno Karabakh', *Ethnopolitics*, Volume 7, No. 4, November 2008, pp. 365–366.

18 Thomas De Waal, *Black Garden: Armenia and Azerbaijan Through Peace and War*, New York: New York University Press, 2003, p. 210.

troops of Armenia in Azerbaijan but that there may be citizens of Armenia who fight as volunteers in Karabakh. However, Human Rights Watch maintains that acquired evidence outweighs such denials, and the organization has even obtained witness accounts on this matter, one of which states:

> An Armenian prisoner of war told Human Rights Watch/Helsinki that he was drafted in the Armenian army at the military commissariat in the Armenian city of Echmiadzin shortly after his release from jail in June 1993, having served time for petty thievery. He was sent with several soldiers from his Armenian army unit, part of the 83rd Brigade based in Echmiadzin, in August 1993 to Hadrut, in Nagorno-Karabakh, where he guarded military vehicles and storehouses. He was captured at the end of August in an ambush near Fizuli, where he had gone with a detail to retrieve grain.

The NGO further describes the involvement of Armenian Armed Forces more extensively and in greater detail, and even concludes that the involvement of the Armenian Armed Forces makes Armenia a party to the conflict "and makes the war an international armed conflict, as between the government of Armenia and Azerbaijan".[19]

Nonetheless, the fact that Armenia has demonstrated a much greater involvement than that of a concerned kin-state from the very beginning of the conflict, and even participated in the war in Nagorno-Karabakh in 1991–1994, does not prove that it is currently engaged in the occupation of the sovereign territory of Azerbaijan. As a matter of fact, the Armenian government continued to try to distance itself publicly from Nagorno-Karabakh, trying to argue that so-called "NKR" is an independent state with independent armed forces, and Armenia has no control over them. Surprisingly, as late as 2016, that was still an issue, and such a position of Armenia was once again publicly confirmed in a Radio Free Europe/Radio Liberty (hereinafter RFE/RL) article by Ron Synovitz that states:

> Armenia's government insists it has not deployed any military subunits on the territory of Nagorno-Karabakh. Both Yerevan and Nagorno-Karabakh's self-declared, internationally unrecognized leadership maintain that the separatist forces solely comprise ethnic Armenian fighters from the breakaway region. But the conclusions of independent Western experts – including researchers for the British Defense

19 Human Rights Watch/Helsinki, *Azerbaijan. Seven Years of Conflict in Nagorno-Karabakh*, 8 December 1994, http://bit.ly/2w3R9q7, pp. 113–127.

Ministry, the International Crisis Group (ICG) and the British-based International Institute for Strategic Studies (IISS) – cast doubt on those claims.[20]

The surprise of the author of this book with such conclusions in the aforementioned year of 2016 will be explained further. However, as Synovitz rightly suggests, the doubts of the "Western experts" are not without solid footing.

The International Crisis Group (hereinafter ICG) has already reported several facts that contradict the Armenian government's narrative as far back as 2004–2005. These reports claimed that despite the support that Nagorno-Karabakh received from the Armenian Diaspora, it remains very much dependent on Armenia's support both economically and militarily. Most of the army of the "NKR" consists of Armenians from Armenia, and senior Armenian authorities openly state that their country supplies military equipment and weaponry to "NKR". Moreover, Armenia delivers a yearly "inter-state" loan to "NKR" that makes up most of the separatist entity's budget.[21] C.W. Blandy, in his paper published by the Defense Academy of the United Kingdom, which used some data from the International Institute for Strategic Studies (hereinafter IISS), states that Armenian Armed Forces have "[s]everal battalions . . . deployed directly in the Karabakh zone on occupied Azerbaijani territory".[22]

What surprises the author is that the aforementioned RFE/RL article still relies on data from independent experts and think tanks, when the issue of the occupation of Azerbaijan's territories by Armenia has already been solved by an international legal body, namely, the European Court of Human Rights (hereinafter ECHR) – in 2015 by its judgment in the *Chiragov and Others v. Armenia* case. In its Grand Chamber judgment, the Court touches upon the relevant international law, and citing Article 42 of Regulations concerning the Laws and Customs of War on Land, The Hague, 18 October 1907 (hereinafter "the 1907 Hague Regulations"), concludes that:

20 Ron Synovitz, *'Open Secret': Experts Cast Doubt On Yerevan's Claims Over Nagorno-Karabakh*, RFE/RL, 5 April 2016, www.rferl.org/a/armenia-nagorno-karabakh-army-synergy/27656532.html.

21 *See* Caspersen, *supra* note 17, p. 367.

22 C. W. Blandy, *Azerbaijan: Is War Over Nagornyy Karabakh a Realistic Option?*, Advanced Research and Assessment Group, Caucasus Series, 08/17, Defence Academy of the United Kingdom, May 2008, www.files.ethz.ch/isn/87342/08_may.pdf, p. 13.

> occupation within the meaning of the 1907 Hague Regulations exists when a state exercises actual authority over the territory, or part of the territory, of an enemy state. The requirement of actual authority is widely considered to be synonymous to that of effective control. Military occupation is considered to exist in a territory, or part of a territory, if the following elements can be demonstrated: the presence of foreign troops, which are in a position to exercise effective control without the consent of the sovereign. According to widespread expert opinion physical presence of foreign troops is a *sine qua non* requirement of occupation, i.e. occupation is not conceivable without "boots on the ground" therefore forces exercising naval or air control through a naval or air blockade do not suffice.[23]

Indeed, occupation is a state when foreign troops on the ground exercise effective control over territory or its parts without the consent of the sovereign state. Further, the Court determines that for the purposes of the case it was deciding it is: "necessary to assess whether [Armenia] exercises effective control over Nagorno-Karabakh and the surrounding territories as a whole".[24] This necessity was explained by the Court as a means to determine Armenia's jurisdiction in the case. Furthermore, ECHR stated that it

> finds it established that the Republic of Armenia, through its military presence and the provision of military equipment and expertise, has been significantly involved in the Nagorno-Karabakh conflict from an early date. This military support has been – and continues to be – decisive for the conquest of and continued control over the territories in issue.[25]

Thus, the Court has also established the "boots on the ground" requirement it referred to in the relevant international law previously cited in its judgment. In paragraph 186 of the case, the Court comes to the definite conclusion that "the 'NKR' and its administration survives by virtue of the military, political, financial and other support given to it by Armenia which, consequently, exercises effective control over Nagorno-Karabakh and the surrounding territories"[26]

23 *Chiragov and Others v. Armenia* [GC], no. 13216/05, ECHR 2015, http://hudoc.echr.coe.int/eng?i=001-155353, para. 96.
24 Ibid., para. 170.
25 Ibid., para. 180.
26 Ibid., para. 186.

As it can be seen from the above, the ECHR has established that since the beginning of the Nagorno-Karabakh Conflict, Armenia has been involved in it militarily and still maintains effective control by means of (but not limited to) its military forces on the ground, and that, in accordance with international law provided by the Court itself, this state of affairs amounts to the occupation of the sovereign territory of Azerbaijan. Despite the fact that ECHR was not asked to give such an evaluation of the situation in the *Chiragov and Others v. Armenia* case, the necessity to establish the facts has enabled the Court to determine the situation on the occupied territories of Azerbaijan on the grounds of international law.

All of the aforementioned shows that there is a clear recognition of the occupation of Nagorno-Karabakh and seven adjacent regions of Azerbaijan by Armenia from the international legal point of view. Unfortunately, the situation on the ground is not reflective of the legal realities. South Caucasus is geopolitically a very complicated region, and failure of international law in this particular case is evident and most likely indirectly linked with the stagnation in geopolitics. Azerbaijan and Armenia as conflicting parties constitute two-thirds of the South Caucasus where the interests of such regional players such as Russia, Iran and Turkey are intertwined into a very tight geopolitical knot, with the outside interest of such international players as the US, the European Union and even Israel.[27] All that creates a very complicated situation of competing interests that only supports the current *status quo* in the Nagorno-Karabakh Conflict, as none of the interested players (with the exception of Azerbaijan) wants to try to loosen the geopolitical knot. Thus, all the attempts at resolution have been failing to date, especially those that have been connected to the enforcement of international law.

Failure of international law: implementation of the UN Security Council resolutions and the right of Azerbaijan to self-defense

Today in the doctrine of international law and international relations there are more and more voices that raise the question of the total failure of international law in the situations of armed conflicts, such as the recent cases of Libya and Syria, and now even Ukraine. That same question has been on the agenda of the UN International Law Commission for some time

27 Kamal Makili-Aliyev, 'Azerbaijan's Foreign Policy: Between East and West…', *IAI Working Papers*, Rome, Italy, No.1305, 2013, www.iai.it/content.asp?langid=2&contentid=834.

now. Nonetheless, the acknowledgment of the failure of implementation and enforcement of international law in the Nagorno-Karabakh Conflict is usually avoided, despite the fact that this conflict is more than a quarter of a century old now and started out long before more recent events in Libya, Syria and Ukraine.

Questions of the effective enforcement of international law are often deadlocked in the international community. Sometimes the goodwill of the states is lacking, sometimes there are not enough resources and sometimes the need for the enforcement is just plain forgotten. In the Nagorno-Karabakh Conflict, the failure of international law occurred precisely because of the deadlocked international community.

From the start of Armenian aggression against Azerbaijan with the aim of annexation of the parts of its sovereign territory, the UN Security Council has adopted four resolutions, mentioned earlier in this chapter, that remain unenforced to this day. In these resolutions, the Security Council actually demands the withdrawal of all occupying forces from the territories of Azerbaijan.[28] Authors who have been analyzing this topic come to similar conclusions.

Heiko Krüger, in his solid work on international law in the Nagorno-Karabakh Conflict, for example, comes to a clear conclusion: "In its resolutions the Security Council demanded . . . that hostilities and the use of force must cease in relation to the acquisition of territories and that occupying forces must be withdrawn".[29] Moreover, he concludes: "there are . . . no reasons to justify the conduct of Armenia, which violates international law. This is also the basic assumption of the resolutions of the UN Security Council and the Council of Europe in which no reference whatever is made to any justifications".[30]

Svante Cornell, in his study of the Nagorno-Karabakh Conflict, when talking about the war enveloping Karabakh in 1993 states that: "It seems as if most actors on the international scene, including the Russians, thought the Armenians had gone too far. In this atmosphere, the UN Security Council passed resolution 822, which called for the withdrawal of . . . forces occupying Kelbajar".[31] This shows that there was a clear intent of the UN Security Council at some point to stop further occupation.

28 Heiko Krüger, *The Nagorno-Karabakh Conflict. A Legal Analysis*, London, New York: Springer, 2010, p. 106.

29 Ibid.

30 Ibid., p. 109.

31 Cornell, *supra* note 3, p. 32.

Shafa Qasimova, summarizing the position of the UN Security Council expressed through its resolutions 822, 853, 874 and 884 of 1993, writes:

> The Council expressed its serious concern at the deterioration of the relations between the Republic of Armenia and the Azerbaijani Republic and reaffirmed the sovereignty, territorial integrity and inviolability of the international border of the Azerbaijani Republic and all other States in the region. The Council demanded immediate cessation of all hostile acts, immediate, complete and unconditional withdrawal of occupying forces from all occupied regions of the Azerbaijani Republic and called for the restoration of economic, transport and energy links in the region, ensuring the return of refugees and displaced persons to their homes.[32]

Thus it is quite obvious that the analysis of the UN Security Council's resolutions provides us with an open and clear message that the Armenian forces conducting occupation should have been withdrawn a long time ago. Moreover, it is commonly known from the UN Charter Article 25 that the Security Council Resolutions are obligatory for implementation by all UN member states,[33] including the Republic of Armenia. However, Armenia to this day ignores these resolutions.

Surprising, in this context, is the fact that the UN Security Council has enough powers to make any state comply with its resolutions. In order to achieve such enforcement from any given state, the Council has to initiate the procedure in accordance with Article 41 of the UN Charter.[34] In other words, it should apply the sanctions of non-military character to the state-violator of its resolutions (for example, complete or partial interruption of economic relations and of rail, sea, air, postal, telegraphic, radio, and other means of communication, and the severance of diplomatic relations). If such sanctions prove to be insufficient to achieve the implementation of its resolutions, the UN Security Council may use military sanctions in accordance with Article 42 of the UN Charter.[35]

Then the question is that maybe the aggression of Armenia was not clear enough for the UN Security Council in the first place, despite its own resolutions that demand the withdrawal of the occupying forces. Let

32 Shafa Qasimova, 'Article 51 of the UN Charter and the Armenia-Azerbaijan Conflict', *Perceptions*, Spring-Summer 2010, p. 83.

33 *UN Charter*, Article 25, www.un.org/en/sections/un-charter/chapter-v/index.html.

34 Ibid., Article 41.

35 Ibid., Article 42.

us take a look at the definition of aggression that can be found in the UN's own documents. A 1974 UN General Assembly resolution provides a clear definition of aggression: "Aggression is the use of armed force by a State against the sovereignty, territorial integrity or political independence of another State, or in any other manner inconsistent with the Charter of the United Nations".[36] Moreover, in its Article 3(a) the aforementioned resolution provides the following:

> Any of the following acts, regardless of a declaration of war, shall, subject to and in accordance with the provisions of article 2, qualify as an act of aggression: (a) The invasion or attack by the armed forces of a State of the territory of another State, or any military occupation, however temporary, resulting from such invasion or attack, or any annexation by the use of force of the territory of another State or part thereof.[37]

These provisions are very straightforward and clear in regards to what aggression actually is under international law. The aforementioned UN Security Council resolutions confirm that the UN Security Council was already aware of the presence of the occupying forces of Armenia in Azerbaijan in 1993. At the same time it has to be pointed out that the provisions of the 1974 UN General Assembly resolution are strong recommendations of the international community to the UN Security Council and in 1993 were still of non-binding character. However, much time has passed, and the Rome Statute of the International Criminal Court of 1998 has emerged, officially making aggression an international crime.[38] Even more importantly, by 2001 it was universally accepted that aggression is an unlawful act and prohibition of such act has acquired the status of *jus cogens* norms.[39] Additionally, in 2015 ECHR confirmed protracted military occupation of Azerbaijan by Armenia, as mentioned earlier in this chapter.

Unfortunately, none of the mentioned facts were considered by the UN Security Council as a reason to make Armenia comply with the Council's

36 UN General Assembly, *Resolution 3314 (XXIX)*, A/RES/29/3314, Article 1, www.un-documents.net/a29r3314.htm

37 Ibid., Article 3(a).

38 *Rome Statute of the International Criminal Court*, 1998, Article 5(1)(d), http://bit.ly/1TeuDLN

39 International Law Commission, *The Report of the International Law Commission*, 53rd Session, GAOR, 56th Session, Supp. No.10 (A/56/10), 2001, pp. 283–284, paras. 4 and 5.

own decisions and start procedures under Chapter VII of the UN Charter, and so the aggression is continuing even today.

Precisely due to the inaction of the UN Security Council, the Republic of Azerbaijan still retains the right of self-defense under Article 51 of the UN Charter that declares:

> Nothing in the present Charter shall impair the inherent right of individual or collective self-defence if an armed attack occurs against a Member of the United Nations, until the Security Council has taken measures necessary to maintain international peace and security.[40]

It has to be pointed out that Azerbaijan recognizes this right in its own legislation, providing in Article 28 of its military doctrine:

> [Azerbaijan] maintains its right to use all necessary means, including application of military force, to restore its territorial integrity according to the norms and principles of international law, if the Republic of Armenia continues to hold under occupation the part of the territory of the Republic of Azerbaijan and refuses to liberate occupied territories in the framework of political resolution of the problem.[41]

Moreover, the state using self-defense is quite free to act on its own discretion. As Yoram Dinstein accurately suggests: "The acting State unilaterally determines whether the occasion calls for the use of forcible measures in self-defence, and, if so, what specific steps ought to be taken".[42] The only requirement that Article 51 requires of a state in question is reporting to the UN Security Council:

> [m]easures taken by Members in the exercise of this right to self-defence shall be immediately reported to the Security Council and shall not in any way affect the authority or responsibility of the Security Council under the present Charter to take at any time such action as it deems necessary in order to maintain or restore international peace and security.[43]

40 *UN Charter*, Article 51, www.un.org/en/sections/un-charter/chapter-vii/index.html

41 *See* Qasimova, *supra* note 32, p. 92.

42 Yoram Dinstein, *War, Aggression and Self-Defence*, New York: Cambridge University Press, 5th ed., 2011, p. 234.

43 *UN Charter*, Article 51, www.un.org/en/sections/un-charter/chapter-vii/index.html.

The only matter that is questionable here is what "until" actually means in the understanding of Article 51 of the UN Charter. Thomas Plofchan examining the limits of right to self-defense as early as in 1992, in connection with the Iraqi occupation of Kuwait in 1990, comes to the solid conclusion that

> an examination of legislative history demonstrates that the framers of the U.N. Charter intended that the right of self-defense should exist at all times unless the Security Council were to specifically prohibit its exercise. . . . The right of self-defense is fundamental and can only be limited if State action is in direct contravention of the purposes and principles of the Charter, or if the Security Council takes explicit action to limit this right.[44]

Malvina Halberstam, tackling the issue in question, similarly concludes that: "It is difficult to believe that some 180 states would have agreed to give up the most fundamental attribute of sovereignty, the right to use force in self-defense, to an international body, and particularly one like the Security Council . . . more plausible interpretation of Article 51 is that a state retains the right of self-defense until the Security Council has taken measures that have succeeded in restoring international peace and security. This interpretation is overwhelmingly confirmed by the legislative history of Article 51".[45]

Thus, until the UN Security Council decides to restore peace and security in the situation of the Nagorno-Karabakh Conflict using means available to it under UN Charter and achieves that goal successfully, Azerbaijan maintains its right to self-defense, provided that it will inform the UN Security Council of the measures it is taking. At the same time, the UN Security Council has set no limitations on Azerbaijan regarding the right of self-defense. With that in mind, all possible actions of Azerbaijan to liberate its territories from occupation should be considered as the exercise of the "inherent" right to self-defense.

Apart from the already mentioned indications of the failure of international law enforcement, there was a change in the framework of conflict resolution itself. The Nagorno-Karabakh Conflict resolution has shifted from the international organization – the UN – to the responsibility of the

44 Thomas K. Jr. Plofchan, 'Article 51: Limits on Self-Defense', *Michigan Journal of International Law*, Volume 13, No. 2, 1992, pp. 372–373.

45 Malvina Halberstam, 'The Right to Self-Defense Once the Security Council Takes Action', *Michigan Journal of International Law*, No. 17, 1996, p. 248.

regional organization – the Organization for Security and Cooperation in Europe (hereinafter OSCE) and its special creation, the so-called "Minsk Group". This questionable move took the UN Security Council even further from acting in the situation of the Nagorno-Karabakh Conflict. Nonetheless, it seems that the UN was quite keen on being able to transfer the Nagorno-Karabakh Conflict as it was already overloaded with conflicts around the world in the beginning of the 1990s. Svante Cornell even speculates that one reason for this decision by the UN may have been a desire to remove Iran from the resolution of the conflict, as Iran, though a member of the UN, was not a member of the Conference on Security and Cooperation in Europe (OSCE's predecessor).[46]

Moreover, a peculiar paradox occurred in the understanding of principles of international law through the political peace process that aims to resolve the Nagorno-Karabakh Conflict since the cease-fire of 1994. To be precise – the paradox is with regard to the understanding of principles of territorial integrity and the right of peoples to self-determination.

Is the right of peoples to self-determination even applicable to the Nagorno-Karabakh Conflict?

The answer to the question posed by this part of the chapter can be summarized as a very short one: no. From the point of view of international law, the right of peoples to self-determination is not applicable to the Nagorno-Karabakh Conflict as a principle, at least not in the broader sense that would then somehow justify secession. However, in order not to make an empty statements, the explanation of international law and the confusion surrounding the right of peoples to self-determination and its applicability to the Nagorno-Karabakh Conflict will follow.

It has to be mentioned that in the process of the resolution of the Nagorno-Karabakh Conflict there are often views expressed that principles of territorial integrity and the right of peoples to self-determination collide with one another and the parties to the conflict argue the superiority of one of the principles over the other. All such claims and views are incorrect by definition. The same goes for the incorrect assumptions on the Armenian side of the conflict that territorial integrity does not mean inviolability of borders.

To start from the roots, it has to be pointed out that the majority of the grounding principles of international law are reflected in the UN Charter and long constitute customary international law (thus they are binding for

46 Cornell, *supra* note 3, p. 116.

all the states in the world). The same applies to the famed principle of territorial integrity.[47] Generally, this principle was included in the UN Charter[48] in 1945 with the aim not to repeat the World War II (and predecessor wars') experience and to prevent the eruption of aggressive and occupational wars of states against each other. The further development of this principle is linked with the 1975 Helsinki Final Act of the then Conference for Security and Cooperation in Europe. This document states:

> The participating States will respect the territorial integrity of each of the participating States. Accordingly, they will refrain from any action inconsistent with the purposes and principles of the Charter of the United Nations against the territorial integrity, political independence or the unity of any participating State, and in particular from any such action constituting a threat or use of force. The participating States will likewise refrain from making each other's territory the object of military occupation or other direct or indirect measures of force in contravention of international law, or the object of acquisition by means of such measures or the threat of them. No such occupation or acquisition will be recognized as legal.[49]

Norms of international law that cover inviolability of borders constitute a part of the principle of territorial integrity, and that is confirmed by the same Helsinki Final Act: "The participating States regard as inviolable all one another's frontiers as well as the frontiers of all States in Europe and therefore they will refrain now and in the future from assaulting these frontiers".[50] In their own turn, such norms require states to: (1) recognize the existing borders as legally binding in accordance with international law; (2) refrain from any territorial claims presently or in future; (3) refrain from any violation of these borders, including threat or use of force for that matter. Thus, the principle of territorial integrity means not only inviolability of borders but an even wider range of sub-principles that include internal matters and not only international relations of the states concerned.[51]

47 Marcelo G. Kohen, in Kohen (ed.), *Secession. International Law Perspectives*, New York: Cambridge University Press, 2006, pp. 6 et seq.

48 *UN Charter*, Article 2(4), www.un.org/en/sections/un-charter/chapter-i/index.html.

49 1975 Helsinki Final Act, 1, IV, www.osce.org/mc/39501?download=true.

50 Ibid., 1, III.

51 Kohen, *supra* note 47, p. 7.

To try to argue that these principles apply to Armenia through international treaty law is quite irrelevant, as all of these norms have constituted customary international law for a long time now and thus are binding on all the states in the world. On the other hand, the argument of the Armenian side is based on the relevance and implementation of the principle of self-determination of the peoples.

The problem with that argument is that such a founding principle of international law as a right of peoples to self-determination in its broader sense, that was reflected in the UN Charter,[52] is in fact a "dead" principle of international law. Moreover, this principle of international law in its broader sense became inapplicable after the decolonization in the 1960s and 1970s. It was included in the UN Charter specifically with the purpose of final abolition of colonialism and imperialism. The Declaration on the Granting of Independence to Colonial Countries and Peoples is particularly significant in this sense. In its paragraph 2 it confirms the decolonization context of the self-determination principle: "All peoples have the right to self-determination; by virtue of that right they freely determine their political status and freely pursue their economic, social and cultural development".[53] At the same time, it adds: "Any attempt aimed at the partial or total disruption of the national unity and the territorial integrity of a country is incompatible with the purposes and principles of the Charter of the United Nations".[54] Basically, indicating that, even in this context, self-determination cannot be a reason for a violation of other principles of international law, namely, territorial integrity.

Such an approach is supported further by the UN Declaration on Principles of International Law, which acknowledges:

> Every State has the duty to promote, through joint and separate action, realization of the principle of equal rights and self-determination of peoples, in accordance with the provisions of the Charter, and to render assistance to the United Nations in carrying out the responsibilities entrusted to it by the Charter regarding the implementation of the principle, in order: a) to promote friendly relations and co-operation among States; and b) to bring a speedy end to colonialism, having due regard to the freely expressed will of the peoples concerned;

52 *UN Charter*, Article 1(2), www.un.org/en/sections/un-charter/chapter-i/index.html.

53 UN General Assembly, *Declaration on the Granting of Independence to Colonial Countries and Peoples*, 1960, A/RES/15/1514, www.un.org/en/decolonization/declaration.shtml, para. 2.

54 Ibid., para. 6.

> and bearing in mind that subjection of peoples to alien subjugation, domination and exploitation constitutes a violation of the principle, as well as a denial of fundamental human rights, and is contrary to the Charter. . . . The territory of a colony or other Non-Self-Governing Territory has, under the Charter, a status separate and distinct from the territory of the State administering it; and such separate and distinct status under the Charter shall exist until the people of the colony or Non-Self-Governing Territory have exercised their right of self-determination in accordance with the Charter, and particularly its purposes and principles.[55]

The Declaration specifically points out the "colonial peoples" and the "speedy end to colonialism". However, by the end of the 1980s and beginning of the 1990s the process of decolonization was long over.

In international legal discourse, similar views are expressed by the proponents of the idea that self-determination was almost entirely limited to the process of decolonization. Although nowadays people who presently do not have a state such as Kurds, Basques or Tibetans invoke the principle of self-determination, and the international community recognizes their demands, nothing is put in motion.[56] Tim Potier even suggests that the Declaration on Principles of International Law itself was already trying "to limit the scope of self-determination from . . . all-embracing 'right'" at the time of its adoption.[57]

Moreover, Nagorno-Karabakh was never a colony, and the Armenian population residing there is in fact a national (ethnic) minority on the territory of the Republic of Azerbaijan and not any kind of "colonial people". Armenians as peoples in the meaning of UN Charter have already exercised their right to self-determination in the Republic of Armenia. In accordance with international law, minorities do not have right to self-determination in a broader sense, due to the fact that their "nation" (people) has already exercised the right to self-determination in their own territory. In the case of the Nagorno-Karabakh Conflict, that territory is the Republic of Armenia.

55 UN General Assembly, *Declaration on Principles of International Law Concerning Friendly Relations and Co-operation among States in Accordance with the Charter of the United Nations*, 1970, A/RES/25/2625, www.un-documents.net/a25r2625.htm.

56 Alexandru-Vlad Crisan, 'The Nagorno-Karabakh Conflict: The Principle of Sovereignty and the Right to Self-Determination', *International Journal of Humanistic Ideology*, Volume 6, No. 2, Autumn/Winter 2015, p. 112.

57 Potier, *supra* note 5, p. 30.

This view is also supported in other prominent international legal doctrine. Heiko Krüger, for example, states:

> What is clear is that neither during the Soviet period nor during the time of the new Republic of Azerbaijan did [population of Nagorno-Karabakh] constitute a separate people of a state. . . . Consequently they were not entitled to the external right to self-determination.[58]

With that in mind, the principle of the right of peoples to self-determination in its broader sense from the legal point of view has no application to the Nagorno-Karabakh Conflict. However, the speculations over this principle are present even today in the framework of negotiations and the peace process. It is evident, then, that this confusion was created by the misinterpretation of international law.

The clear stance of international law that minorities do not have right to self-determination (unlike peoples in the meaning of the UN Charter) was solidified in 1984 by the UN Human Rights Committee, which is charged with monitoring the International Covenant on Civil and Political Rights, in its CCPR General Comment No. 12.[59] It was even further clarified by the CERD Committee in its General Recommendation No.21, in paragraph 2:

> The International Covenant on Civil and Political Rights provides for the rights of peoples to self-determination besides the right of ethnic, religious or linguistic minorities to enjoy their own culture, to profess and practice their own religion or to use their own language.[60]

Thus, the UN Committees clearly distinguish between the rights of peoples to self-determination and minority rights.

Moreover, Heiko Krüger in his analysis clearly stated that "customary international law assumes that the right to self-determination is granted primarily to the 'peoples'".[61] Joshua Castellino, tackling the topic of the right of peoples to self-determination and its applicability to peoples, indigenous peoples and minorities, confirms the distinction between indigenous

58 Krüger, *supra* note 28, pp. 55–56.

59 *CCPR General Comment No. 12: Article 1 (Right to Self-determination)*, The Right to Self-determination of Peoples, 13 March 1984, www.refworld.org/docid/453883f822.html

60 *CERD General Recommendation XXI (Right to Self-determination)*, 23 August 1996, para. 2.

61 Krüger, *supra* note 28, p. 54.

peoples and minorities. He writes that their specific differentiation with respect to the fact that the former possess the right to self-determination and the latter do not is readily accepted in law as well as in literature.[62] Moreover, Castellino in his analysis concludes that minorities can claim self-determination in a non-political sense as a guarantee of human rights and access to special measures but do not enjoy self-determination as a right in a broader (political) sense.[63]

Thus, in the case of the Nagorno-Karabakh Conflict, the principle of self-determination under international law can be applied only in a more narrow sense to the self-determination of minorities in cultural, religious and linguistic matters, unlike the right to self-determination provided initially by the UN Charter, which applies only to "peoples".

The norms reflected in the Helsinki Final Act are only supportive of that position:

> The participating States will respect the equal rights of peoples and their right to self-determination, acting at all times in conformity with the purposes and principles of the Charter of the United Nations and with the relevant norms of international law, including those relating to territorial integrity of States. By virtue of the principle of equal rights and self-determination of peoples, all peoples always have the right, in full freedom, to determine, when and as they wish, their internal and external political status, without external interference, and to pursue as they wish their political, economic, social and cultural development. The participating States reaffirm the universal significance of respect for and effective exercise of equal rights and self-determination of peoples for the development of friendly relations among themselves as among all States; they also recall the importance of the elimination of any form of violation of this principle.[64]

Specifically due to the fact that "peoples" can exercise their right to self-determination without going outside the norms of international law on territorial integrity of the states, it can be pointed out that the Helsinki Final Act of 1975 (one of the grounding legal instruments of OSCE) has endorsed the principle of self-determination in its narrow (internal) sense.

62 Joshua Castellino, 'International Law and Self-Determination. Peoples, Indigenous Peoples and Minorities', in Christian Walter, Antje Von Ungern-Sternberg and Kavus Abushov (eds.), *Self-Determination and Secession in International Law*, Oxford University Press, 2014, p. 38.

63 Ibid., p. 41.

64 1975 Helsinki Final Act, 1, VIII, www.osce.org/mc/39501?download=true

Apart from OSCE's progressive Act of 1975, the same view is expressed by the UN CERD Committee in the aformentioned General Recommendation No.21, in paragraph 4, which states:

> The right to self-determination of peoples has an internal aspect, that is to say, the rights of all peoples to pursue freely their economic, social and cultural development without outside interference. In that respect there exists a link with the right of every citizen to take part in the conduct of public affairs at any level, as referred to in article 5 (c) of the International Convention on the Elimination of All Forms of Racial Discrimination. In consequence, Governments are to represent the whole population without distinction as to race, colour, descent or national or ethnic origin.[65]

Further in the text of the General Recommendation, the Committee attaches this aspect to minorities:

> In order to respect fully the rights of all peoples within a State, Governments are again called upon to adhere to and implement fully the international human rights instruments and in particular the International Convention on the Elimination of All Forms of Racial Discrimination. Concern for the protection of individual rights without discrimination on racial, ethnic, tribal, religious or other grounds must guide the policies of Governments. In accordance with article 2 of the International Convention on the Elimination of All Forms of Racial Discrimination and other relevant international documents, Governments should be sensitive towards the rights of persons belonging to ethnic groups, particularly their right to lead lives of dignity, to preserve their culture, to share equitably in the fruits of national growth and to play their part in the Government of the country of which they are citizens. Also, Governments should consider, within their respective constitutional frameworks, vesting persons belonging to ethnic or linguistic groups comprised of their citizens, where appropriate, with the right to engage in activities which are particularly relevant to the preservation of the identity of such persons or groups.[66]

65 *CERD General Recommendation XXI (Right to Self-determination)*, 23 August 1996, para. 4.
66 Ibid., para. 5.

As can be seen, the UN CERD Committee also acknowledges the existence of the internal aspect of self-determination that can be applied to minorities. Despite that fact, it concludes its General Recommendation with a disclaimer:

> The Committee emphasizes that, in accordance with the Declaration on Friendly Relations, none of the Committee's actions shall be construed as authorizing or encouraging any action which would dismember or impair, totally or in part, the territorial integrity or political unity of sovereign and independent States. . . . In the view of the Committee, international law has not recognized a general right of peoples unilaterally to declare secession from a State.[67]

As it can be seen, the UN CERD Committee is also mindful of the principle of territorial integrity and does not want to jeopardize its solidity by allowing misinterpretations of its recommendations. On the other hand, it also raises an important question: does the right of peoples to self-determination, even in a broader (external) sense, mean an automatic right to secession? The Committee itself believes that international law has not recognized such a right, and it has to be pointed out that the majority of scholars generally agree with the point of view of the Committee.

Heiko Krüger points out that many legal authors (referencing them) reject the rights to secession and that neither international treaties nor customary international law pertaining to state practice provide a solid basis for such rights, excluding the cases of colonialism, situations of foreign occupation or where national law or national agreements allow secession.[68] Tim Potier, on the other hand, when faced with the same question, provides solid analysis and openly argues in this line of logic: "Does a right of secession 'unquestionably' 'exist'? . . . I do not think so. I am not sure that . . . 'secession' will ever exist in international law or ever can. . . . If 'secession' became a right it would undoubtedly threaten not just international peace and security but the international framework as a whole".[69]

The author has to agree with aforementioned scholars that self-determination as a right *per se* does not mean a right to secession. However, the

67 Ibid., para. 6.

68 Heiko Krüger, 'Nagorno-Karabakh', in Christian Walter, Antje Von Ungern-Sternberg and Kavus Abushov (eds.), *Self-Determination and Secession in International Law*, Oxford University Press, 2014, p. 220.

69 Potier, *supra* note 5, p. 36.

possibility of the existence of such a right in the case of Nagorno-Karabakh will, nonetheless, be examined further, even without its connection to the principle of self-determination. This is done in order to retain the comprehensive nature of legal arguments provided in this book.

Right to secession or quasi-legal excuses: legitimacy and status of so-called "NKR"

Despite the fact that there are no peoples in Nagorno-Karabakh to claim a right to self-determination and somehow justify secession, there are still arguments coming from the separatists that so-called "NKR" has become an independent state using its right to secession provided by the Soviet legislation for the autonomous regions, including former NKAO.[70]

However, a close examination of the Soviet legislation shows a different picture. The USSR Constitution of 1977 in its Article 72 provided that each Union Republic (Armenia and Azerbaijan were such republics before the dissolution of USSR) shall retain the right to freely secede from USSR. Moreover, in Article 76 it explicitly states that a Union Republic is a sovereign Soviet Socialist state that has united with other Soviet Republics in the Union of Soviet Socialist Republics. Furthermore, the former NKAO, it appears, was not a "sovereign" and according to Articles 82 and 86 of the aforementioned constitution was a constituent part of the Union Republic; in our case, the Azerbaijan Soviet Socialist Republic. In addition, Article 78 of the 1977 USSR Constitution provides that the territory of the Union Republic may not be altered without its consent. Even the boundaries between Union Republics could have been changed only by their own mutual agreement and any such agreement would be subject to ratification by the USSR.[71]

However, in 1990, on the brink of the dissolution of the USSR, the Law on Procedures for Resolving Questions Related to the Secession of Union Republics from the USSR (hereinafter Law on Secession) was adopted. This law provided in its Article 3:

> In the Union republic that has within it autonomous republics, autonomous provinces and autonomous regions, the referendum shall be

70 For example, *see* note verbale dated 21 March 2005 from the Permanent Mission of Armenia to the United Nations Office at Geneva and the UN High Commissioner for Human Rights, E/CN.4/2005/G/23, pp. 7 et seq.

71 Potier, *supra* note 5, pp. 39–40.

> held separately in each autonomous unit. The peoples of autonomous republics and autonomous formations shall retain the right to decide independently the question of staying in the USSR or in the seceding Union republic, as well as to raise the question of their own legal state status. In a Union republic whose territory includes areas with concentration of national groups that make up the majority of the population in a given locality, the results of the voting in these localities shall be considered separately during the determination of the referendum result.[72]

This particular piece of legislation is being used by the separatists in Nagorno-Karabakh and the Armenian government to justify the creation of "NKR". While it is true that the Law on Secession was adopted in the Soviet Union, it has many legal problems with both its existence and implementation. First, as it can be seen from this discussion, it clearly contradicts the superior legal act – the 1977 Constitution of the USSR – and thus, it was unconstitutional by definition. Second, as Tim Potier points out, this law was adopted in an attempt to slow down, at the time, the momentum of the secession of the Baltic States and only later became relevant to other union republics.[73]

Legal researchers who have studied and analyzed the text of the law and that of the 1977 Constitution of the USSR point out that in addition to the mentioned contradictions, the law itself was not implemented properly, and the requirements of this law were not properly met. Heiko Krüger, for example, argues that in accordance with the 1977 Constitution of USSR, the autonomy that Nagorno-Karabakh had was understood as a cultural autonomy, related mostly to the minority's use of language and culture and not a territorial autonomy *per se*. It also lacked elementary qualities of statehood, unlike union republics. Concluding his analysis of the 1977 Constitution of the USSR, Krüger states:

> [T]he 1977 Constitution of the USSR did not grant Nagorno-Karabakh a right to secession that it could have successfully exercised. Territorial alterations were solely in the hands of the union republics or the USSR, which, however, upheld the status quo of Nagorno-Karabakh.

72 Hurst Hannum, *Documents on Autonomy and Minority Rights*, Dordrecht: Martinus Nijhoff, 1993, p. 754.

73 Potier, *supra* note 5, p. 40.

Furthermore, his analysis of the law revealed that the procedure envisioned by the Law on Secession for the autonomous entities such as NKAO should have been coupled with its union republic – namely, the Azerbaijan Soviet Socialist Republic. However, none of the union republics, including Azerbaijan, have performed such a procedure. Moreover, none of the criteria set out by the Law were satisfied by the NKAO, including timing of the referendum, joint commissions, time frames for formal secession procedure, etc. Krüger proves that the referendum carried out by separatists in NKAO on 10 December 1991 was not valid, as even with "a valid referendum Nagorno-Karabakh could not have completed an effective secession from the Azerbaijan SSR on its own".[74]

Krüger during his analysis even states:

> The 1990 Law on Secession finally installed a procedure that regulated a process for the exercise of the right to secession pursuant to Art. 72. However . . . the Law on Secession provided for such a complex, cumbersome and disadvantageous procedure which would not only have a successful secession delayed for years but could even have made it impossible. Kohen and Cassese therefore take the view that the Law on Secession was one of the final acts with which Gorbachev attempted to prevent the foreseeable premature dissolution of the USSR.[75]

This is especially important, as the truth of the matter is that the procedure under the 1990 Law on Secession was so complicated and required so many years to implement that none of the former Soviet Union republics has successfully implemented it, taking into account that the USSR effectively ceased to exist on 26 December 1991. Tim Potier agrees, stating: "In truth, no union republic seceded 'lawfully', according to the terms and 'conditions' enshrined in the Law on Secession".[76] That, in turn, means, that the Azerbaijan Soviet Socialist Republic became an independent state by virtue of the dissolution of Soviet Union, and under the principle *uti possidetis juris*, Nagorno-Karabakh was a constituent part of a new Republic of Azerbaijan. Heiko Krüger comes to similar conclusions while discussing Soviet legislation.[77]

In her study of the *uti possidetis* principle in regard to problematic situations in the post-Soviet space, Anne Peters concludes the following:

74 Krüger, *supra* note 28, pp. 28–39.
75 Ibid., p. 32.
76 Potier, *supra* note 5, p. 41.
77 Krüger, *supra* note 28, p. 37.

> [O]lder administrative lines stemming from the pre-independence era (e.g. Soviet era) cannot be opposed against the currently existing "mother" states (e.g. CIS states) if they are not acknowledged in *their* domestic law as it stands, too. Neither does *uti possidetis* apply on the basis of factual control over a territory, in the absence of a formal administrative line.[78]

That fair conclusion when implemented into the discussion of the Nagorno-Karabakh Conflict means that the Nagorno-Karabakh separatists can't argue that because Azerbaijan did not have total control over Nagorno-Karabakh in the turbulent times of the USSR's dissolution, the *uti possidetis* principle did not apply to Nagorno-Karabakh as part of the territory of Azerbaijan.

Interestingly, even the proponents of the independence of so-called "NKR" agree that the arguments under the 1990 Law on Secession are less than credible. For example, William Slomanson suggests:

> [Nagorno-Karabakh] abandon its exclusive reliance on its interpretation of the . . . 1990 Soviet statute. . . . There is no multilateral treaty on secession. There never will be. That would be political suicide. An alternative source of international law – state practice – does not provide an expedient yardstick for measuring the legitimacy of unilateral secessions. . . . [T]he right to self-determination does not include a general right to secession".[79]

Moreover, Slomanson advises against using the case of Kosovo as well, due to the fact that the International Court of Justice did not consider the questions of statehood and right to secession of Kosovo.[80]

That basically brings us to the one point left to cover, to answer the question of the current status of the so-called "NKR". The arguments that come from the Armenian government and the Nagorno-Karabakh separatists are related to the recognition of the separatist entity in Nagorno-Karabakh. These claims can be summarized as stating that in accordance with the Montevideo Convention of 1933, the self-proclaimed so-called

78 Anne Peters, 'The Principle of Uti Possidetis Juris. How Relevant Is It for Issues of Secession?', in Christian Walter, Antje Von Ungern-Sternberg and Kavus Abushov (eds.), *Self-Determination and Secession in International Law*, Oxford University Press, 2014, p. 136.

79 William R. Slomanson, 'Nagorno Karabakh: An Alternative Legal Approach To Its Quest For Legitimacy', *Thomas Jefferson Law Review*, Volume 35, No. 1, 2012, p. 41.

80 Ibid., p. 42.

"Nagorno-Karabakh Republic" should be recognized on the international level. However, in accordance with Article 1 of the Montevideo Convention – which states that "[t]he state as a person of international law should possess the following qualifications: a) a permanent population; b) a defined territory; c) government; and d) capacity to enter into relations with the other states" – the aforementioned claims become rather groundless on closer examination.

It so happens that the territories occupied by the Republic of Armenia that have created a separatist entity there include much more than just a territory of the Nagorno-Karabakh (former NKAO) itself. It also includes seven more adjacent regions of Azerbaijan. As was discussed earlier in this chapter, the fact of the occupation was proven beyond any doubt by the *Chiragov and Others v. Armenia* case in 2015. Moreover, this case was already used by the ECHR as a precedent to pass judgment in another case, *Muradyan v. Armenia*,[81] becoming a solid part of its case law. The ECHR once again confirms that the separatist entity survives by virtue of the will of the Republic of Armenia.[82] It is thus unclear where the separatists would draw borders. In general, it is impossible to talk about clearly defined borders where there are shaky lines of contact between two military forces.

Additionally, a permanent population is out of question as well. The separatist regime has never defined its population and has not introduced clear "citizenship", which is of course impossible without clearly defined territory. If we consider the attempts to claim the population that is right now *de facto* residing on the occupied territories, it is further unclear why that does not include the Azerbaijani population that was forced out and ethnically cleansed from these territories. The fact that the Azerbaijani population was forcefully expelled from the occupied territories is quite well known, but in order to use a neutral data source, a simple fact-check on CIA World Factbook website will reveal that the Factbook estimates 580,000 internally displaced persons (IDPs) from Karabakh and indicates that the Nagorno-Karabakh separatist region is populated almost entirely by ethnic Armenians.[83] Such *status quo* clearly speaks of the impermanence of the population.

81 *Muradyan v. Armenia* [GC], no. 11275/07, ECHR 2016, http://hudoc.echr.coe.int/eng?i=001-168852, para. 126.

82 Ibid.

83 *The World Factbook 2017*. Washington, DC: Central Intelligence Agency, 2017, http://bit.ly/2fo0iiJ.

The government is nonexistent by definition – the so-called "Nagorno-Karabakh Republic" is practically fully administrated by the Republic of Armenia. It would be very strange to talk about independent administration of the "NKR" taking into account the full subordination of the separatist entity (both politically and financially) to the Armenian kin-state.[84] Finally, taking into account the fact that not a single state in the world (including Armenia)[85] has recognized that separatist entity, there cannot be any capacity of so-called "NKR" to enter into relations (namely, diplomatic) with any other subjects of international law.

As it can be seen from this discussion, the so-called "NKR" does not in any way qualify as an independent state and cannot be treated even as a *de facto* state or a state-like entity.

Concluding remarks

This chapter has covered the main questions of international law in the Nagorno-Karabakh conflict. It is quite obvious that Armenia in the Nagorno-Karabakh Conflict has the role of an occupying power rather than of a concerned kin-state. It has used the opportunity provided by the dissolution of the Soviet Union to annex its neighbor's territories under a pretext of defending interests of the Armenian community in Nagorno-Karabakh, and together with Armenian separatists has established a regime that is supposed to play the role of the *de facto* state aspiring to full statehood and international recognition.

The arguments that are used to justify such behavior include the right of peoples to self-determination and the subsequent right to secession, claiming that NKAO has seceded from Azerbaijan legally under the Soviet legislation and that so-called "NKR" is a *de facto* state. As can be seen from this chapter's discussion, these arguments are proven to be without grounds or justification under international law. The right of peoples to self-determination is inapplicable to the Nagorno-Karabakh Conflict in a broader sense and does not give rise to a subsequent right to secession. All of the occupied territories are part of Azerbaijan under international law.

That being said, the interests of the Armenian population of Nagorno-Karabakh cannot be disregarded in any case or point of time. In fact, the Armenian population that resides in Karabakh is a minority on the territory

84 *Chiragov and Others v. Armenia* [GC], no. 13216/05, ECHR 2015, http://hudoc.echr.coe.int/eng?i=001-155353, paras. 169–186.

85 Slomanson, *supra* note 79, p. 39.

of Azerbaijan that has rights to internal self-determination, basically allowing for autonomous cultural, linguistic and economic development without jeopardizing the territorial integrity of Azerbaijan. The international community knows some successful cases of autonomies blossoming in their home countries and even receiving preferential treatment. One such case is the Aland Islands.

2 International law in the Aland Islands precedent

The Aland Islands precedent is one of the few examples of a serious territorial conflict between states with a clear ethno-political dimension that found a peaceful resolution under international law. That resolution was the result of the strong support of the international community and the clear dedication of the parties to the conflict to finding common ground for resolution of the conflict under the international law. This precedent created an example that demonstrates many of the best international practices of good governance that have been studied, analyzed and implemented in the international community. This chapter is dedicated to the analysis of elements of international law in the Aland Islands precedent that might be helpful in the resolution of the Nagorno-Karabakh Conflict. The analysis will attempt to identify the unique features of the precedent and show what makes it a special case in international law and for the international community.

While the history of the Aland Islands is interesting in itself and can be easily traced to the Stone Age,[86] only a brief historical overview will be needed in this chapter to provide the historical context (rather than a comprehensive analysis in historical terms) of the conflict that led to the creation of the precedent. The analysis will concentrate on such fundamental parts of the precedent as demilitarization and neutralization zones in the Aland Islands, legal aspects of such zones under international law, the international legal basis for the autonomy of the Aland Islands and a discussion of minority rights – with a specific focus on cultural, linguistic and educational rights of the minority group living in the autonomy as well as the right to domicile. The analysis will intentionally avoid focusing on the relations of the Aland Islands autonomy and the European Union (hereinafter the EU), as such a legal discussion, though undoubtedly important

86 Matts Dreijer, *The History of the Åland People. I:1 From the Stone Age to Gustavus Wasa*, Mariehamn, 1986, pp. 17–50.

DOI: 10.4324/9780429353437-2

and interesting, is less relevant for the topic in comparison to the aforementioned issues of public international law. Thus, the questions of the Aland Islands and the EU will be mentioned only as needed for the comprehensiveness factor of general arguments set forth by this chapter.

In addition, this chapter will discuss legal aspects of the resolution of the conflict around the Aland Islands between Sweden and Finland, specifically its settlement by the League of Nations, concentrating on the stronger points of the involvement of universal international organizations in the context of conflict resolution. Such features of the settlement as the establishment of specific commissions, their inquiries and opinions and the value of the informed decision based on facts and scholarly opinion will be discussed in the context of international law implementation. Furthermore, the effect that such implementation can carry throughout the centuries will be analyzed further.

The Aland Islands of strategic importance: a brief historical overview

Historically, the Aland Islands have been considered of strategic importance for a very long time due to their geographic location in the Baltic Sea region and their role in the European great power politics. The islands themselves constitute an archipelago of approximately 6,500 small and very small islands. The total area of the archipelago is roughly 13,517 km² with 89 percent of it covered by water. A century ago the population consisted of 20,000.[87] The population of the area is around 29,789 people as of the end of 2018,[88] the majority of whom reside on the main island. Throughout its history, the majority of the population of the islands was Swedish.

Three different periods of modern history are important to understanding the importance of the Aland Islands. The first period is that of Swedish rule over the islands that stretched from 1157 and to 1809. The second period is that of Russian rule between 1809 and 1917, and the third period is Finland's sovereignty over the Aland Islands from 1917 up to the present.[89] Swedish dominion over the islands, the beginning of which coincided with the rise of Valdemar the Great to the absolute monarchy in the Danish kingdom,[90] was

87 Unto Vesa, 'The Åland Islands As a Conflict Resolution Model', in *Territorial Issues in Europe and East Asia: Colonialism, War Occupation, and Conflict Resolution*, Northeast Asian Foundation, 2009, p. 36.

88 Statistics Finland, *Finland in Figures 2019*, Helsinki: Grano Oy, 2019, http://bit.ly/2K2ggyV, p. 10.

89 James Barros, *The Aland Islands Question: Its Settlement by the League of the Nations*, New Haven and London: Yale University Press, 1968, p. 1.

90 Dreijer, *supra* note 86, p. 266.

marked by an aggressive and successful foreign policy of Sweden (especially in the XVII century) that allowed the country to effectively rule the Baltic Sea. Sweden was later, in the XVIII century, challenged by the rising Russia, which occupied the Aland Islands for the first time in 1714. Russians quickly turned the islands into a naval base to attack the coast of Sweden. Nonetheless, after years of struggle, the Aland Islands returned to the jurisdiction of Sweden in 1721 under the Peace Treaty of Nystad, along with the whole of Finland.[91]

Later in the XVIII century, Sweden lost most of the wars with Russia, while the latter gained most of the territory of Finland by the middle of that century. The Aland Islands with the rest of Finland were incorporated into the Russian Empire in 1809 after the military campaign it waged with the consent of Napoleon, gained at the Congress of Erfurt in 1808. The subsequent Treaty of Frederikshamn confirmed the fact that the islands would remain under the sovereignty of the Russian Empire, which had started to fortify the islands and used their strategic importance as a military base against Sweden, as a defense point of newly acquired Finland and, even more importantly, as a game piece in domination over the Gulf of Bothnia. During the XIX century, the threat to Russian ambitions of domination in the Baltic Sea came not from Swedes but from the British, who destroyed Russian fortifications in the Aland Islands in the mid-XIX century during clashes in the Baltic Sea. Nonetheless, the British failed to achieve a strategic objective with this move. They were not able to persuade Sweden to join the war with Russia.[92]

Despite the proposals from the British and the French, Sweden refused to occupy the Aland Islands after Russian troops were cleared from their base there. Instead, in 1856 after the end of Crimean War, at the peace negotiations in Paris, the Swedish position was based on the restitution of the islands and neutralization of their territory as of an independent state under the protection of France, Britain and Sweden.[93] That bid of Sweden failed. However, the Convention on Demilitarization of the Aland Islands was adopted between Britain, France and Russia. The specific nature of the treaty was that it was permanent in character – meaning that even in the event of change of sovereign rule over the islands, the demilitarized status could not be altered.[94] This situation very accurately reflected the interests of European powers in the Baltic Sea. The demilitarization of the islands

91 Barros, *supra* note 89, p. 1.

92 Ibid., pp. 2–6.

93 Ibid., pp. 6–8.

94 Gunnar Jansson, 'Introduction', in Lauri Hannikainen and Frank Horn (eds.), *Autonomy and Demilitarisation in International Law: The Åland Islands in a Changing Europe*, Kluwer Law International, 2007, p. 2.

was hampering Russian domination over the Baltic Sea and specifically over the Gulf of Bothnia, which suited the interests of Britain and France. In return, Russians were allowed to keep sovereignty over the islands.

Moreover, the Convention on Demilitarization became a part of the larger Paris Peace Treaty (in the form of Article 33), which ended the Crimean War. Sweden itself was excluded from the agreements reached by France, Britain and Russia, and the matter was settled for the next 50 years. Then the Russians violated the restrictions imposed on them by the Convention in 1906, landing troops in the archipelago, establishing a station there and patrolling waters with naval units; all of this was done under the pretext that the internal situation in Russia created the necessity to prevent arms smuggling. In 1907–1908 Russia tried to use diplomacy to abrogate the Convention of 1856 and be released from obligations concerning the Aland Islands, but that attempt failed due to the resistance from Britain and Sweden. Further tensions did not occur until the beginning of World War I.[95]

At the beginning of the World War I, Sweden tried to maintain its neutrality to the best of its ability, rejecting the proposal of Germany to join at her side for the promise of restoration of Swedish sovereignty over the Aland Islands. In response, Germany rejected the proposal of Sweden to allow the Aland Islands to remain neutral for the duration of the war, given the Russian consent to that. German activities in the Baltic Sea soon started to threaten Russia to the point that it began contemplating the fortification of the Aland Islands, fearing German occupation of the archipelago. Russia had communicated its desire to do so to Sweden first, in order not to steer Swedes into the German orbit of influence. The reaction from Sweden was positive, due to the lack of choice mostly. Sweden, however, was not able to extract a promise from Russia not to use the Aland Islands militarily after the World War I was over.[96]

When World War I was finally coming to an end, the tensions around the Aland Islands stirred once again. While the Aland Islands belonged to the Russian Empire they had been considered a part of Finland, as they were included in the empire together in the early XIX century. Finland gaining its independence in 1917 raised the issue of the Aland Islands in light of the turmoil in Russia and with European powers engaged in World War I. Finland considered the islands its sovereign territory, while islanders had a different view. In 1917, 7,000 people of the population of the Aland Islands signed a petition to reunite with Sweden. Their desire was actively

95 Barros, *supra* note 89, pp. 11–19.
96 Ibid., pp. 20–30.

supported by Sweden, which was concerned for the population there and also for the strategic value of the Aland Islands. In 1918, the Finnish side invaded the islands, prompting the Swedish troops to make a landing there under the pretext of a "humanitarian mission". Swedish troops were forced to leave after the German occupation of the islands in March of 1918, which ended with the defeat of Germany in World War I.[97]

The Finnish-Swedish tensions were rising due to the clear desire of Sweden to assist the Aland Islands in their bid for independence and subsequent reunification with Sweden.[98] On the other hand, the civil war in Finland as well as the general turmoil and uncertainty of the post-World War I situation did not play into the confidence of the Aland Islands' population in Finland and their self-security. Their fears were based on the domination of Finnish culture and language as opposed to the islanders being Swedish, both linguistically and culturally, and firmly oriented toward Sweden economically. Moreover, the population of the islands feared that Finland might end up socialist or communist in the political sphere.[99]

By the time of the Paris Peace Conference of 1919, Sweden and Finland were already engaged in the full-fledged territorial conflict. However, during the course of the Paris Peace Conference, the differing positions of the European centers of power and those of Finland and Sweden led to a situation where the conflict could not be resolved during the Conference itself. Instead, the matter was referred to the newly created League of Nations on a proposal from Britain as "the only course for the Alanders".[100]

As can be seen from this discussion, the historical background of the Aland Islands is rich with clashes of European powers trying to use the strategic value of the islands for their own interests. Nonetheless, after the Paris Peace Conference, the Aland Islands moved into one of the most important periods of their history, a period that made them into an example and a special case in many areas, specifically due to the decision that was made by the League of Nations. That decision and its consequences will be discussed next.

97 Pertti Joenniemi, 'The Åland Islands Issue', in Clive Archer and Pertti Joenniemi (eds.), *The Nordic Peace*, Ashgate, 2003, p. 88.

98 Barros, *supra* note 89, pp. 89–100.

99 Joenniemi, *supra* note 97; Jansson, *supra* note 94, p. 3.

100 Barros, *supra* note 89, p. 210.

League of Nations breakthrough: the settlement of the Aland Islands question

As the great powers were not able to reach a consensus on the Aland Islands question and the Paris Peace Conference did not resolve the issue,[101] Finland was been prompted to grant the Aland Islands some measure of autonomy in hopes of reducing the separatist tensions of the islands' population.[102] The Autonomy Act of 1920 that granted the Aland Islands the autonomy by Finland was prepared by the Finnish governmental committee that was supposed to develop a system of regional decentralization of Finland. However, the committee ended up applying the self-government structures only to one specific region of the country – the Aland Islands. Despite the fact that the committee's work was based on a comparative analysis and its thorough work on the Act, the Alanders, who were not consulted and did not participate in the making of the Act, rejected the arrangement by Finland.[103]

Moreover, in the same month the Autonomy Act of 1920 was adopted by Parliament, the Alanders once again appealed to the King and government of Sweden for the reunion of the Aland Islands and Sweden. The Finnish government reacted immediately with the prime minister coming to the Aland Islands and presenting the Autonomy Act there while threatening in a speech drastic consequences should the Alanders fail to accept the Act. During the meeting, the councilors, as a protest against the prime minister's speech, began to leave the premises. Shortly after that, some of the members of the separatist movement in the Aland Islands were detained. Such a turn of events soured relations between Finland and Sweden until the decision by the League of Nations.[104]

Once the League of Nations was charged with the resolution of the question, Sweden requested that the future of the Aland Islands should be decided through a plebiscite by its population. However, no such popular vote was organized. Moreover, the local population or their representatives were not participating in the League of Nations process to any significant extent, and main negotiations went on between Finland, Sweden and the

101 Vesa, *supra* note 87, p. 44.

102 Barros, *supra* note 89, p. 216.

103 Markku Suksi, 'Prosperity and Happiness through Autonomy. The Self-government of the Åland Islands in Finland', in Yash Ghai and Sophia Woodman (eds.), *Practicing Self-Government. A Comparative Study of Autonomous Regions*, Cambridge University Press, 2013, p. 63.

104 Christer Janson, 'The Autonomy of Aland: A Reflection of International and Constitutional Law', *Nordisk Tidsskrift International Ret*, No. 51, 1982, p. 16.

Council of the League of Nations.[105] Finland and Sweden were able to present their positions clearly to the Council. While Sweden defended the right of Alanders to opt for reunification with Sweden, Finland strongly argued that the case was a domestic affair and the Aland Islands being a part of Finland did not constitute an entity (with its population) that could enjoy the right to self-determination.[106]

Ultimately, the League of Nations established two commissions to deal with the issue. The first one, the Commission of Jurists, analyzing the issue of self-determination, came to the following conclusion:

> [The] principle recognizing the rights of peoples to determine their political fate may be applied in various ways; the most important of these are, on the one hand the formation of an independent State, and on the other hand the right of choice between two existing States.[107]

It also concluded that the issue was not domestic one and that the League of Nations was competent to deal with the case, which was regarded as points in favor of the Swedish position on the question.[108]

The Commission of Jurists based its conclusions on several points of international law applicable at the time. It suggested that the principle of self-determination should be brought into line with the protection of minorities, as both have a similar subject, such as the development of social, ethnical or religious characteristics of a given group or population. Moreover, it suggested that a compromise solution should be based on the extensive grant of liberty to the minorities in accordance with the norms of international law and in the interest of peace. The Commission of Jurists further pointed to the necessity to take into account the actual situation in the Aland Islands in terms of relative homogeneity of the population residing there, the geographical location and the racial, linguistic and cultural links between the Aland Islands and Sweden as well as the forcible separation of the Islands from Sweden in the beginning of the XIX century. Using this line of argument, the Commission of Jurists concluded that the Aland Islands question cannot be considered a question of domestic jurisdiction of Finland under public international law. Moreover, it was a question that

105 Suksi, *supra* note 103, pp. 63–64.
106 Vesa, *supra* note 87, p. 45.
107 Suksi, *supra* note 103, p. 64.
108 Vesa, *supra* note 87, p. 45.

the League of Nations was competent to solve under Article 15 paragraph 4 of the Covenant of the League of Nations.[109]

Nonetheless, the Commission of Jurists did not have an opinion on the actual substance of the issue of the validity of the right to self-determination in the case of the Aland Islands. Armed by the recommendations of the Commission of Jurists, the Council of the League of Nations then decided to establish an inquiry Commission of Rapporteurs to study the merits of the case and closely examine the facts. After extensive study and a comprehensive inquiry on all aspects of the question, the Commission of Rapporteurs submitted detailed analysis of the case to the Council of the League of Nations that included such conclusions as: 1) geographically the Aland Islands are a continuation of the Finnish mainland; 2) politically the islands have been part of Finland since 1809 and before that Swedish sovereignty regarded them under Finnish provinces; 3) legally the Aland Islands were under Finnish sovereignty and all States (including Sweden) recognized the independence of Finland with no reservations concerning Finnish borders.[110]

Moreover, the Commission of Rapporteurs concluded that the right of sovereignty of Finland over the Aland Islands is incontestable and that detachment of the islands from Finland would be an alteration of the legal status of Finland that would deprive the country of a part that belongs to it. The Commission also suggested that a minority (or any fraction of the population) does not have the right to secession *per se*, as that would be a threat to the order of the state as it will cause its destabilization. Furthermore, promoting secession can become a reason for anarchy in international life and presents a theory that is incompatible with the established idea that a state constitutes a political and territorial unity. The only exception, the Commission of Rapporteurs suggested, was that minority separation is justified as the last resort measure when a state is unwilling or unable to enact and apply just and effective guarantees for the minority. However, the Commission of Rapporteurs was not able to find any evidence of any serious violations of the rights of the population of the Aland Islands and thus, it saw no immediate reasons to recommend secession or a plebiscite on the question of the Aland Islands. Instead, it recommended a comprehensive solution based on the maintenance of sovereignty of Finland, but only if specific conditions (that will be discussed further) were met. If Finland was to fail to meet those conditions and the expectations of the Commission of Rapporteurs, then it proposed the secession of the Aland Islands from

109 Suksi, *supra* note 103, pp. 64–65.
110 Vesa, *supra* note 87, pp. 45–46.

Finland based on the referendum that would be conducted by the population there.[111]

The conclusions of the Commission of Rapporteurs became the basis for the resolution of the Aland Islands question. Finland and Sweden agreed on the conditions of the settlement before the final decision of the Council on 24 June 1921 of the League of Nations that enshrined the principles of the Aland Islands settlement. Three days later, Finland and Sweden confirmed their formal agreement to the settlement.[112] The decision to support the settlement was not easy, however, for Sweden or for Finland. Herbert A.L. Fisher, the British representative to the League of Nations at the time of the settlement of the Aland Islands question, after the settlement was reached, wrote:

> We have reached a settlement, not without difficulty, for both the Swedes and the Finns were very obstructive, of the Aland islands question and the settlement is so intrinsically just and fair and is so obviously in the interests of European peace, that I have little doubt that it will stand... Indeed, it is clear to me now that the dispute could never have been settled by the ordinary means of diplomacy.[113]

Indeed, the League of Nations has reached a breakthrough that had a concrete result and laid the ground for a special precedent in international law.

It is also important to discuss some of the specifics of the settlement that laid out a very thorough set of guarantees to the Aland Islands, as was envisioned by the conclusions of the Commission of Rapporteurs. The important part of the settlement was that general regulations in the form of principles were later transformed into more specific regulations in the form of actual norms. The principles reflected in the agreement between Sweden and Finland had covered the obligations of Finland to assure and guarantee the preservation of language and culture and local Swedish traditions to the population of the Aland Islands.

These principles were to be integrated into the Autonomy Act of 1920 in the form of six specific guarantees recounted in the decision of the Council of the League of Nations:

> 1) The Landsting and the Communes of the Aland Islands shall not in any case be obliged to support or to subsidize any other schools

111 Suksi, *supra* note 103, p. 65.

112 Barros, *supra* note 89, pp. 329–333.

113 Ibid., p. 333.

than those in which the language of instruction is Swedish. In the scholastic establishments of the State, instruction shall also be given in the Swedish language. The Finnish language may not be taught in the primary schools, supported or subsidized by the State or by the commune, without the consent of the interested commune; 2) When landed estate situated in the Aland Islands is sold to a person who is not domiciled in the Islands, any person legally domiciled in the Islands, or the Council of the province, or the commune in which the estate situated, has the right to buy the estate at a price which, failing agreement, shall be fixed by the Court of First Instance (Häradsrätt) having regard to current prices. Detailed regulations will be drawn up in a special law concerning that act of purchase, and the priority to be observed between several offers. This law may not be modified, interpreted, or repealed except under the same conditions as the Law of Autonomy; 3) Immigrants into the Aaland archipelago who enjoy rights of citizenship in Finland shall only acquire the communal and provincial franchise in the Islands after five years of legal domicile. Persons who have been five years legally domiciled in the Islands shall not be considered as immigrants; 4) The Governor of Aland Islands shall be nominated by the President of the Finnish Republic in agreement with the president of the Landsting of the Aland Islands. If an agreement cannot be reached, the President of the Republic shall choose the Governor from a list of five candidates nominated by the Landsting, possessing the qualifications necessary for the good administration of the Islands and the security of the State; 5) The Aland Islands shall have the right to use for their needs 50% of the revenue of the land tax, besides the revenues mentioned in Article 21 of the Law of Autonomy; 6) The Council of the League of Nations shall watch over the application of these guarantees. Finland shall forward to the Council of the League of Nations, with its observations, any petitions or claims of the Landsting of Aland in connection with the application of the guarantees in question, and the Council shall, in any case where the question is of juridical character, consult the Permanent Court of International Justice.[114]

114 Sarah Stephan, 'The Autonomy of Åland Islands', in Sia Spiliopoulou Åkermark (ed.), *The Åland Example and Its Components – Relevance for International Conflict Resolution*, Mariehamn: Åland Islands Peace Institute, 2011, pp. 30–31; *The Åland Agreement in the Council of the League of Nations*, Minutes of the Seventeenth Meeting of the Council, June 27th, *League of Nations Official Journal*, September 1921, p. 201.

These guarantees have been transformed by Finland into the domestic law by amending the Autonomy Act of 1920 with the Guaranty Act of 1922. Basically, Finland incorporated the decision of the Council of the League of Nations into the Guaranty Act of 1922, and the Aland Islands use institutions according to the Autonomy Act of 1920.[115] The details of the Aland Islands autonomy and its progression to this day, however, are a separate subject that requires analysis.

The Aland Islands of self-governance: autonomy and its features

In addition to the guarantees discussed earlier, the Aland Islands have received additional rights within their autonomy. Those rights included participation in municipal and regional elections, eligibility for office, acquisition of real estate in accordance with a specific law, rights of trade and exemption from general duties to perform military service.[116] It is generally understood though, that the Autonomy Act was complete with the adoption of the law in 1938. This law regulated the procedure of the acquisition of real estate located on the islands by the non-resident of the Aland Islands and its acquisition back by the residents of these islands.[117]

The autonomy of the Aland Islands has been growing and developing since the League of Nations settlement. The Guaranty Act of 1922 was in force until it was replaced by the new Autonomy Act of 1951 that incorporated all the previous guarantees (except for the supervisory role of the League of Nations, which no longer existed) and added new ones. The next update took place in 1991 when the Autonomy acquired another set of new features. It has to be noted that in 2010, the Aland Islands government started preparations for the next proposal of revision of the Autonomy Act in order to reflect new realities such as globalization, development of the society, the Finnish Constitution of 1 March 2000 and European integration.[118]

The Autonomy Act of 1951 was a considerable development in terms of legal provisions reflected in the new legislation on the Aland Islands. The jurisdiction of the Legislative Assembly of the Aland Islands was considerably enlarged and concretized. Moreover, this Act has introduced a status of "regional citizenship" providing for the so-called "right of domicile"

115 *See* Suksi, *supra* note 103, p. 66; Stephan, *supra* note 114, p. 32.
116 Ibid.
117 Janson, *supra* note 104, p. 18.
118 Stephan, *supra* note 114, p. 32.

that belongs to persons permanently residing in the islands. The residence period of five years in the Aland Islands was a prerequisite for the right of domicile. Only persons who have acquired such rights had access to the full set of rights enjoyed specifically by the Alanders. For example, the right to vote, to own real estate and possibly to own an enterprise. Moreover, now if the treaty that was ratified by Finland came into conflict with the Autonomy Act of the Aland Islands, the conflicting provisions of such a treaty would only enter into force in the islands if the Legislative Assembly formally agreed to that. Reinforcing the autonomy of the Aland Islands has allowed Finland to mitigate the negative effect of the concern of the Aland Islands that was created by the disappearance of the supervisory body – the League of Nations.[119]

The current status of the autonomy of the Aland Islands, however, is defined by the Autonomy Act of 1991. This Act further expands the autonomy of this self-governing territory. It adds new conditions for the acquisition of the right of domicile. Apart from five years of residency, the sufficient proficiency in Swedish is now required for a permanent residency. In addition, the Autonomy Act of 1991 applies more restrictions to the right to acquire real estate on the islands, introduces more favorable provisions for the islanders to appoint their Governor and introduces the role of the Aland Islands in negotiations conducted by Finland with other states to conclude any treaty. The only deviation from the original guarantees of the Autonomy Act of 1920 is that restrictions on the teaching of the Finnish language in primary schools without the consent of the commune concerned have been lifted, and the Finnish language can be taught freely as a foreign language. Schools need to get the commune's approval if they want to apply a language of instruction other than Swedish.[120]

The Aland Islands' system of self-governance has interesting features that include solid and strong institutions native to the islands and combined bodies that provide links of this system to the state of Finland. Prominent features include delimitation of powers and checks and balances with regard to the Finnish state institutions. Thus, working in parallel, the Legislative Assembly of the Aland Islands and the Parliament of Finland can adopt legislation in specified areas of jurisdiction. The same logic is applied to the executive bodies of Government of the Aland Islands and

119 Lauri Hannikainen, 'The International Legal Basis of the Autonomy and Swedish Character of the Åland Islands', in Lauri Hannikainen and Frank Horn (eds.), *Autonomy and Demilitarisation in International Law: The Åland Islands in a Changing Europe*, Kluwer Law International, 2007, pp. 62–63.

120 Ibid., p. 64.

the Government of Finland, each playing their own role in administration. At the same time, the boundaries of roles of Governor of Aland, Aland Delegation and the President of Finland are specified in less detail. Due to the centralized nature of the Finnish judiciary, the knowledge of the laws of the Aland Islands is required of all courts in the country, while the Aland Islands feature their own specific Administrative Court.[121]

The autonomy itself is very non-restrictive when it comes to institutions. The Autonomy Act of 1991 (hereinafter Autonomy Act) does not specifically regulate the institutions of the autonomy, leaving that to the acts of the Legislative Assembly of the Aland Islands. Moreover, the Act points out that in all matters of autonomy the Legislative Assembly, elected by the direct and secret ballot by the population of the islands with the right of domicile, is a representative body. All the matters of internal structures of the self-government of the Aland Islands are decided by the Legislative Assembly that adopts proper legislation regarding such matters, and in addition, in regard of all matters concerning areas of education, social affairs, health and environment. The Aland Islands have two fundamental acts that cover the creation of structures of its government: one that deals with the organization of the Legislative Assembly of the Aland Islands and one that deals with the Government of the Aland Islands.[122]

The act on organization of the Legislative Assembly, better known as the Rules of Procedure, determines that there are 30 members of the Assembly that are elected for a four-year period at a time. The rights to vote for the candidates to the Assembly belong to Finish citizens with the right of domicile in the Aland Islands. Interestingly, the right to vote in municipal elections was extended to foreign citizens in 1995, while the residence requirement to vote in municipal election was lowered to one year in 2006.[123] The party system in the Aland Islands traditionally differs from the party system in mainland Finland, with connections drawn only between social-democrats. The difference is in the status of the political association. The parties in Finland are registered as such, while political groups in the Aland Islands are registered as public associations. At the same time, the Rules of Procedure stipulate that the relations of the Legislative Assembly and the Government of the Aland Islands are grounded in the principle of parliamentarism. This means that the Government has to be accountable for the benefits of the confidence of the Assembly.[124]

121 Stephan, *supra* note 114, p. 33.
122 Suksi, *supra* note 103, p. 82.
123 Stephan, *supra* note 114, pp. 34–35.
124 Suksi, *supra* note 103, p. 83.

The development and protection of the autonomy of the Aland Islands is always the highest point of its political agenda, and the Legislative Assembly pays special attention to the issues of status of the islands both in Finland and in accordance with international law. There is even a special Committee on Autonomy that functions in the Assembly that is charged with advisory role on questions about the constitutional rights of the Aland Islands, their external relations and even EU affairs. Government of Aland Islands can consult the Committee as needed. Nonetheless, the broad legislative powers of the Assembly are not competitive with those of the Parliament of Finland. While the Finnish Constitution applies in the islands, the legislation passed by the Finnish Parliament concerning the areas that are in the competence of Legislative Assembly, does not. Even if Legislative Assembly was not able to adopt a certain legislation, its Finnish counterpart is not applicable automatically, making two systems profoundly distinct from each other.[125]

A wide range of legislative authority of the Assembly as stipulated by Section 18 of the Autonomy Act of 1991 includes municipal administration, public order and security, building and planning, tenancy and rent regulation, the protection of nature and environment, historical heritage, healthcare, social welfare, education, farming, forestry and fisheries, postal services, traffic and trade. The Aland Islands have a limited taxation competence that includes the additional tax for income on the islands, provisional extra income tax, trade and amusement taxes, municipal taxes.[126] Other taxes are levied by the state, while autonomy itself is financed through the system of tax equalization in form of 0.45 percent of the income of the state for the year in question, excluding state loans. Nonetheless, it is for the Legislative Assembly to decide how to spend this money in the local budget. However, the change of the taxation system, by the transfer of the taxation competence from the state to the autonomy, is reflected in the recommendations on the amendments proposed for the Autonomy Act.[127]

Legislative powers of the autonomy are quite flexible and have the possibility to adapt to the changes in the legislation of the state through the establishment of norms that in substance are in conformity with Finnish legislation. So when the matters that fall to the competence of both the Aland Islands and the state arise, the Legislative Assembly can react with adopting legislation that in principle is in the competence of the state, but

125 Stephan, *supra* note 114, p. 35.

126 *Act on the Autonomy of Åland* (1991/1144), www.finlex.fi/en/laki/kaannokset/1991/en19911144.pdf, sec. 18.

127 Stephan, *supra* note 114, p. 36.

in substance does not deviate from it. This is made to ensure the uniformity and clarity of the legislation and sometimes is achieved through introduction of template legislation in the Aland Islands that basically implements the new legislation of the state into the autonomy.[128]

The Government of Aland is composed first by the election of the First Minister who in turn proposes the composition of the government, which requires a simple majority vote of the Assembly. This government in turn can be removed by the no-confidence vote of an absolute majority of 16 members, making the system non-symmetrical. The Government of the Aland Islands has an apparatus of different offices and administrative bodies, while its members serve as heads of different departments and participate in making of administrative decisions.[129] The state also maintains public offices in the Aland Islands capital, Mariehamn. They are limited to the tax authorities, population register and the Administrative Court. The Aland Islands as an autonomy maintain their own public health services and police force as well as the administration of around 16 municipalities.[130] The municipal self-government is a constitutional right in Finland, and municipalities have their own guaranteed right to taxation, but the competence to regulate this taxation belongs to the Legislative Assembly. Municipalities of Aland are more restricted in terms of functions if compared to the municipalities of mainland Finland.[131]

Another important position is the Governor of Aland. He is appointed by the President of Finland under prior agreement with the Speaker of the Legislative Assembly or from the list of candidates provided by the Assembly if the President and the Speaker fail to come to an agreement. The role of the Governor is quite flexible and inconsistent and cannot be related to the heads of regional administrations in Finland. The Governor represents both the President of Finland in the Aland Islands and the Government of Finland itself. The Governor opens and closes the sessions of the Legislative Assembly, attends to matters of state security in the islands and serves as a speaker to the Aland Delegation, that is a very important institution with the supervisory function over Aland Islands' legislation. [132]

The Aland Delegation was initially created by the Autonomy Act of 1921 to ensure fair and just determination of tax equalization for the financing of the Aland Islands. After the process of revisions of the autonomy status,

128 Ibid.
129 Suksi, *supra* note 103, p. 83.
130 Stephan, *supra* note 114, pp. 38–39.
131 Suksi, *supra* note 103, pp. 83–84.
132 Stephan, *supra* note 114, p. 41.

the powers of the Aland Delegation have grown. It is an independent body of four experts (two elected by the Legislative Assembly and two appointed by the Finnish Government) that have important duties not only concerning taxation but also in the legislative process and as advisory both to the state and to the autonomy, especially in matters of conflict of authority.[133]

The judicial powers in the Aland Islands belong to the state, and two state courts exercise their jurisdiction in the islands. The Court of First Instance deals with civil and criminal matters, while administrative cases are dealt with by the Administrative Court. Appeals are treated in the mainland. Nonetheless, the courts in the Aland Islands apply legislation of both the Legislative Assembly, as well as of the Parliament of Finland,[134] where the Aland Islands maintain one elected member as their representative.

The Aland Islands of peace: demilitarization and neutralization

As previously discussed, the Aland Islands have always been regarded as strategic due to their geographic location and in terms of military dominance in the Baltic Sea. Hence, their demilitarized status has served as a compromise and safeguard of peace and stability between European states since the mid-XIX century. At the same time, demilitarization and non-fortification have functioned well during times of relative peace in the Baltic Sea and were strongly challenged during times of world wars raging in Europe when the demilitarized status of the Aland Islands was violated several times.[135]

Nonetheless, demilitarization and neutralization are among the most prominent features of the autonomy of the Aland Islands and have a long history under public international law. It is clearly stipulated that the population of the islands is probably the most interested party in the monitoring of the demilitarized and neutralized regime, despite the fact that the defense concerns of the Finnish state are somewhat obscure for the autonomy of the Aland Islands. Still, concerns of the Aland Islands are subject of public debate in various contexts and thus, the questions of demilitarization and neutralization continue to develop in the public agenda.[136] With that in

133 Ibid., p. 42.
134 Suksi, *supra* note 103, p. 84.
135 Vesa, *supra* note 87, p. 50.
136 Sia Spiliopoulou Åkermark, 'Ålands Demilitarisation and Neutralisation: Continuity and Change', in Sia Spiliopoulou Åkermark (ed.), *The Åland Example and Its Components – Relevance for International Conflict Resolution*, Mariehamn: Åland Islands Peace Institute, 2011, p. 52.

mind, demilitarization and neutralization are not losing their topicality for the development of the autonomy of the Aland Islands and should not be considered a "settled case" – solidified and static.

The terminology of demilitarization and neutralization has to be cleared, though. Allan Rosas suggests

> [by] *demilitarisation* is usually meant that the territory in question is free from permanent military installations and forces, while *neutralisation* implies the additional obligation to keep the territory outside war operations in time of armed conflict (but with a possible right of the State exercising sovereignty over the neutralized territory to bring in troops as a defensive measure).

At the same time, in modern international legal terminology a confusion may arise, as sometimes demilitarized zones in the armed conflict reflect the substance of the neutralized territory under the definitions provided. Moreover, neutrality of the state and neutralization of territories can also be subjects of controversy in the modern understanding of these terms.[137] Hence, here it seems more adequate to use these terms in a classic sense, as provided by Rosas.

In these particular terms, the demilitarization and neutralization regime of the Aland Islands is founded on four main international treaties that indicate not only the status of the regime but its development as well. As was mentioned before in this book, in 1856 France, Great Britain and Russia agreed on what is modernly known as the Convention of the Demilitarization of the Aland Islands that provided demilitarized status for the islands after the Crimean War. In 1921 the Convention on the Non-fortification and Neutralization of the Aland Islands was adopted (also known as Aland Convention 1921). This treaty established a demilitarization and neutralization regime in the Aland Islands in conjunction with the resolution of the Aland Islands question by the League of Nations. Further, in 1940 the Treaty between Finland and the Soviet Union concerning the Aland Islands was adopted in Paris. In 1948 a diplomatic letter from the USSR to Finland reaffirmed the validity of this treaty, while in 1992 another reaffirmation followed from Russian Federation. The Peace Treaty of Paris of 1940 in its Article 5 confirmed the demilitarized status

137 Allan Rosas, 'Åland Islands as a Demilitarised and Neutralised Zone', in Lauri Hannikainen and Frank Horn (eds.), *Autonomy and Demilitarisation in International Law: The Åland Islands in a Changing Europe*, Kluwer Law International, 2007, pp. 23–24.

of the Aland Islands. Apart from demilitarization and neutralization, this treaty gave a right to Russia to have a consulate on the Aland Islands.[138]

While the 1856 treaty, sometimes referred to as "Aland servitude", established a provision that limited Russia in its sovereignty with the obligation not to fortify or establish and retain any kind of facility of military or naval nature on the islands,[139] it only concerned a small group of European powers, leaving, for example, Sweden outside the scope of the treaty. In 1921, however, the spectrum on the states covered by the effects of the treaty was expanded considerably, covering the majority of Baltic Sea littoral states.[140]

The legal arguments around all four of these international treaties can be summarized as covering: a) the continued validity of these documents, b) if they are still in force and c) their interpretation. For example, the 1921 Convention envisions in its wording that its norms will remain in force despite any changes in the *status quo* of the Baltic Sea. At the same time, a majority of legal experts are also supportive of the idea that the 1921 Convention remains in force.[141] Still, the signatories of the treaty exclude Lithuania, Norway and Russia and their obligations under this treaty were also debated in terms of customary international law. The treaty itself is the most substantive treaty out of all four, which increases its importance. It features several very prominent points: 1) obligations imposed on Finland not to fortify the Aland Islands; 2) demilitarized zone of the islands is geographically established with corresponding coordinates; 3) demilitarized status of the islands is detailed and provides specific exceptions; 4) there is a confirmation of the "right of free passage" in the text of the treaty; 5) neutralization regime is also confirmed with exceptions; 6) there are guarantees of monitoring and implementation of the treaty.[142]

The exceptions of military nature that the 1921 Convention provides, however, are not exceptions from the general rule. They were supposed to be implemented only with the purpose of strengthening the demilitarization and neutralization regime of the Aland Islands. In this sense the defense policy and concerns of Finland have different logic when it comes to the Aland Islands.[143] Defending national borders and the special regime of the Aland Islands thus differ in logic and implementation.

138 Åkermark, *supra* note 136, p. 53.
139 Barros, *supra* note 89, pp. 10–11.
140 Åkermark, *supra* note 136, p. 53.
141 Rosas, *supra* note 137, pp. 25–26.
142 Åkermark, *supra* note 136, p. 54.
143 Rosas, *supra* note 137, p. 31.

The problems also arise when it comes to the boundaries of the demilitarized zone in the sense that coordinates provided in 1921 have inconsistencies as compared to modern cartography. General rules still being that demilitarized zone consists of territories of the Aland Islands and their territorial waters of three nautical miles. Nonetheless, the clarification of the boundaries and methods of such clarification are still high on Finland's agenda in regard to the Aland Islands and its status as a demilitarized zone.[144]

Another controversy arises from the right of passage provided by the 1921 Convention in terms of whether such a right is applicable to warships passing through territorial waters of the Aland Islands. The doctrine seems to be split on the issue. While on one hand the treaty that regulates public international law at the sea makes no distinction between military and civilian vessels, there are arguments that the exercise of right of passage by military vessels in the Aland Islands contradicts the intent of the demilitarization regime in the first place. State practice shows that Finland, Sweden and even Russia have softened their views on this issue in the overall framework of the demilitarization regime.[145]

More questions have been asked about the interpretation of norms such as those established by the 1921 Convention, for example, the right of Finland to visit the Aland Islands with light surface warships from time to time and be anchored on the islands temporarily. The issue was already controversial at the time of its adoption, further stirring some concerns from the authorities of the Aland Islands about the frequency of such visits from the Finnish Navy. Ultimately, the issue was settled through the Governor of Aland, who would serve as a liaison between the Ministry of Defense of Finland and the Government of the Aland Islands. The Finnish Coast Guard (part of the Border Guard Service) had also raised some questions. While it is a service under the Ministry of Interior and not the Ministry of Defense, until 1980 its vessels were considered warships and only later on received a status of "other public vessels". The fact that the Finnish Coast Guard is not under direct military command and carries light weapons indicated that they are lawful under the provisions of demilitarization and neutralization regime. The state practice of parties to the treaty is also indicative of the recognized lawfulness of Finnish Coast Guard.[146]

Despite all the questions raised in connection to the demilitarization and neutralization regime of the Aland Islands, it has clearly been able

144 Åkermark, *supra* note 136, pp. 58–60.
145 Ibid., p. 63.
146 Rosas, *supra* note 137, pp. 32–33.

to survive for a very long time. Such a situation is indicative of its deep entrenchment in the international law and requires some discussion of the customary international law and Article 8 of the 1921 Convention that deals with the longevity of the norms of this treaty. Interestingly, the general discussion in scholarly works seems to indicate that general opinion on this issue is quite monolithic.

Rosas, for example, citing Suontausta, Rotkritch, Bring, Fagerlund, Hannikainen and others, comes to the conclusion that "[t]here is a wide body of opinion suggesting that at least the main principles of the demilitarization regime have achieved status of customary law". He ultimately arrives at the conclusion that all of the four treaties that constitute the demilitarization and neutralization regime of the Aland Islands are still in force, and their main elements are part of customary international law.[147] It is hard to disagree with him and with the range of international legal scholars that he cites, simply because state practice has seen continued respect for the regime, even from the Baltic Sea littoral states that were not part of the aforementioned treaty law, such as Lithuania, Norway and Russia, with no recorded incidents in practice to show otherwise.

The same opinion is expressed by another notable authority on the Aland Islands precedent, Sia Spiliopoulou Åkermark, who stated: "The regime is viewed . . . as customary law binding on the parties to the chain of treaties that have confirmed the regime over centuries". This link to customary international law is also self-explanatory in terms of the longevity of the provisions of 1921 Convention, which in Article 8 ensures that its provisions on demilitarization and neutralization shall remain in force regardless of which country the Aland Islands shall belong to in the future. This logic is fully in sync with the provisions of Article 62 of the Vienna Convention on the Law of Treaties of 1969 in regard to treaties that define borders. This means that if a change in sovereignty takes place in case of the Aland Islands, the state that acquires sovereignty over the islands cannot claim a fundamental change in circumstances and automatically assert invalidity of the treaty.[148] Thus, even states that are not under the obligation of the 1921 Convention – if they should gain sovereignty over the Aland Islands – will also be bound by the obligations to maintain the demilitarization and neutralization regime in the islands until and unless this condition is renegotiated with other relevant states in the Baltic Sea.

Åkermark raises another fair question in the problematic of the demilitarization and neutralization regime in the Aland Islands. The international

147 Ibid., pp. 28–29, 35.
148 Åkermark, *supra* note 136, pp. 68–69.

guarantor functions of the League of Nations have not passed to the UN in the course of history. That leaves mainly Finland and other signatories of the treaty to oversee its function. However, the need for military capabilities to defend the demilitarization and neutralization regime is unquestionable. As Åkermark indicates, the scholarly opinion seems to be in agreement that the main obligation to guarantee the regime lies with Finland, as a state exercising sovereignty over the islands and for as long as it exercises such sovereignty.[149] It is perhaps a paradox that a state charged with ensuring the regime of demilitarization is obligated to do so by military means without jeopardizing the regime itself. Nonetheless, the demilitarization and neutralization regime is an important feature of the Aland Islands precedent.

The Aland Islands of rights: minority rights in the autonomy

The Aland Islands precedent has another very prominent feature – minority rights. When the Aland Islands question was decided by the League of Nations in 1921, one of the main issues troubling the population of the Aland Islands (and its kin-state Sweden) in modern terms was endangerment of cultural, educational and linguistic rights.[150] One of the features of the resolution provided by the League of Nations was that the Swedish language will be taught at schools and will generally be an official language in the Aland Islands.[151] However, the minority rights regime in the Aland Islands has grown considerably since the beginning of the XX century due to the development of international law on minorities and Finnish law as well as the obligations of Finland as a sovereign state. The modern situation with cultural, educational and linguistic rights in the Aland Islands is discussed further now.

As the official language of the Aland Islands is Swedish, it is first necessary to take a look at the general situation of the Swedish-speaking minority in Finland. Swedes constitute the largest minority in Finland, and their minority rights regime is considered a model one in the international legal doctrine. The Swedish language is constitutionally given an official status on par with Finnish. The whole Swedish-speaking population of Finland can be described as split into two regimes: population of the Aland Islands in their cultural and territorial autonomy and the other part of the population located on the mainland Finland that acquired rights based on

149 Ibid., p. 70.
150 Jansson, *supra* note 94, p. 3.
151 Vesa, *supra* note 87, p. 47.

territorial and personal principles. In mainland Finland, the right to use one's own language is dependent on the municipality or commune in question, creating a system with unilingual Finnish or Swedish communes or bilingual communes with a majority that is either Finnish-speaking or Swedish-speaking.[152] Under the provisions of the current Autonomy Act, the official language of the Aland Islands is Swedish, making this region of Finland unilingual. Interestingly, the provision making the Swedish language official was not included into the previous acts on autonomy and the Swedish language was used *de facto*.[153]

The language of instruction in all of the Aland Islands' schools is historically Swedish. At the same time, most of the Swedish-speaking population of the islands do not know how to speak Finnish. Despite that fact, recently the number of students that learn the Finnish language in schools has grown considerably, as opposed to the previous decades in the Aland Islands' history. The Finnish-speaking population of the islands, in contrast, has a good command of Swedish mainly because it is obligatory to learn Swedish in the Finnish-speaking schools of the mainland Finland.[154]

Despite the fact that the definition of the "minority" in international law is still debated, the principal features and criteria have been clarified for some time now. The Swedish-speaking population of the Aland Islands clearly fits the definition of the minority under international law[155] that has a strong determination to maintain the islands' monolingual, Swedish-speaking territory.[156] The population of Aland Islands was successful in doing so by, basically, maintaining all the schools as Swedish. No Finnish schools were ever created in the islands. Before the adoption of the Autonomy Act of 1991, there was considerable debate that lasted for decades and involved arguments that the international treaty law on the minorities that Finland has adopted contradicted the restrictive nature of

152 Frank Horn, 'Minorities in Åland with Special Reference to their Educational Rights', in Lauri Hannikainen and Frank Horn (eds.), *Autonomy and Demilitarisation in International Law: The Åland Islands in a Changing Europe*, Kluwer Law International, 2007, pp. 151–154.

153 Heidi Öst, 'The Cultural and Linguistic Safeguards of the Åland Minority Protection regime', in Sia Spiliopoulou Åkermark (ed.), *The Åland Example and Its Components – Relevance for International Conflict Resolution*, Mariehamn: Åland Islands Peace Institute, 2011, p. 75.

154 Lauri Hannikainen, *Cultural Linguistic and Educational Rights in the Åland Islands. An Analysis in International Law*, Helsinki: Publications of the Advisory Board for International Human Rights Affairs, No. 5, 1992, p. 15.

155 Horn, *supra* note 152, p. 153.

156 Hannikainen, *supra* note 154, p. 21.

the linguistic rights regime in the Aland Islands. The debate involved the autonomy in the islands and the Finnish Government itself. However, the Autonomy Act of 1991 settled the issue cementing the Swedish language as official and giving legislators in the Aland Islands more control over education in the autonomy. At the same time, it is argued that the Autonomy Act of 1991 simultaneously weakened the provisions on the language of education in the Aland Islands.[157]

The Autonomy Act of 1991 has also provided the possibility for the graduates of schools in the Aland Islands to be admitted to state-owned or sponsored higher education institutions and to graduate from them. However, while theoretically graduates from Aland Islands' schools who lack necessary Finnish language capacity for admittance have to be exempted from this restriction in higher education institutions of Finland, in practice most of them are enrolling to Swedish universities and schools. Because proficiency in Finnish is required for a wide range of employment opportunities in Finland, the minority guarantees for the Aland Islands population may have had a negative effect in the sense that they are restricting the options of Alanders in mainland Finland.[158] Another side of the story is that despite the constitutional guarantees that Finnish and Swedish languages are equal, as should be their implementation and maintenance, the Swedish-speaking population generally is not satisfied with the language services provided by the state. This happens mostly due to the fact that in practice Swedish skills of Finnish-speaking civil servants and public sector employees are quite weak and insufficient.[159] This however, does not preclude the Aland Islands' population from enjoying the use of their language on the territory of the autonomy – rather its makes their lives harder in terms of communication and relations with mainland Finland.

It is also important to view the minority rights of the population of the Aland Islands through the prism of the international human rights law and specific treaties that relate to minority rights protection and how they apply to the Aland Islands. It has to be pointed out that the first priority for the UN in the middle of XX century was firm establishment of the regime of non-discrimination of all persons, and minority rights lacked specific attention until the middle of the 1980s. The conventions of this period have main themes of equality and non-discrimination and in order to ensure the rights of groups, it is allowed to use affirmative action in the form of

157 Öst, *supra* note 153, pp. 78–80.
158 Ibid., pp. 80–81.
159 Horn, *supra* note 152, p. 155.

differential treatment, but only as a temporary measure. Language was, of course, one of the grounds for discrimination that was prohibited.[160]

One of the most important provisions on minority rights that relates to the Aland Islands precedent in the documents of that period is Article 27 of the Covenant on Civil and Political Rights that recognized the rights of minorities to practice their religion, use their own language and enjoy their own culture.[161] Unsurprisingly, this provision does not provide any guarantees beyond the basic rights enjoyed by the majority, restricting the scope of norms it created to basic equality and non-discrimination. Thus, the interpretation of the norms of international human rights law has been in the hands of international bodies that have somewhat clarified the lawfulness of the affirmative action or positive discrimination. For example, in the Belgian Linguistics case of 1968, the European Court of Human Rights, interpreting the prohibition of discrimination under Article 14 of the European Convention on Human Rights, held that there is a need for objective and reasonable justification for the deviation from principle of equality and it should pursue a legitimate aim. Moreover, between the means employed and the legitimate aims sought there is supposed to be a reasonable relationship of proportionality.[162]

As Hannikainen points out, despite the fact that the Swedish language has exclusive status in the Aland Islands, it was never criticized by the international human rights bodies as discriminatory toward other languages for several reasons. For one, Finnish-speaking residents in the Aland Islands never demanded special rights for use of language in the name of equality and, in principle, special rights of the Swedish-speaking community do not violate the criteria set out by the European Court of Human Rights.[163] Frank Horn, analyzing similar questions, adds to this argument, stating:

> Assuming that special self-administrative regimes created for minorities at the State level should benefit from special protection, the increase in numbers of the local minority formed by members of the State majority may not result in this group achieving as generous minority guarantees as the local majority".

160 Hannikainen, *supra* note 154, p. 27.

161 UN General Assembly, *International Covenant on Civil and Political Rights*, General Assembly resolution 2200A (XXI), 1966, http://bit.ly/1Oq5JFt

162 *Case "Relating To Certain Aspects Of The Laws On The Use Of Languages In Education In Belgium" v. Belgium*, no. 1474/62; 1677/62; 1691/62; 1769/63; 1994/63; 2126/64, 1968, http://hudoc.echr.coe.int/eng?i=001-57525.

163 Hannikainen, *supra* note 154, pp. 28–29.

He also notes that Finnish-speakers seem to be accepted as part of the Aland Islands population in full regard and tend to assimilate. Moreover, there does not seem to be a viable Finnish-speaking community in the Aland Islands.[164] With that said, the Aland Islands minority rights regime does not infringe the rights of Finnish-speakers due to the fact that they do not constitute a minority within minority in the Aland Islands and do not express interest in additional rights. Nor do they feel threatened by the Swedish-speaking environment.

Moreover, the autonomy provisions for the Aland Islands that have solidified in the Act of Autonomy and subsequent legislation are protecting the culture and language in the islands through regulations of land and property acquisition as well. The right of domicile, that was discussed earlier, played a very important role in this process. It has restricted the possibility of acquisition of real estate property in the Aland Islands for non-permanent residents and provided the right of redemption to the residents of the Aland Islands.

Apart from that, the land acquisition rights have been more and more restricted with the revisions of the autonomy legislation. Between the Autonomy Acts of 1951 and 1991, land acquisition procedure on the islands has been tied to the permissions of the Government of the Aland Islands and the inheritance-based exceptions in the laws have been narrowed to cover only direct descendants and surviving spouses. Despite the fact that this regime became stricter than what it was when originally agreed to by Sweden and Finland, the international acceptance followed, and it was especially evident with regard to the relations with the EU. When Finland joined the EU, its accession treaty even featured an additional protocol that guarantees the Aland Islands that their autonomous provisions in this area will not be threatened or prejudiced by EU regulations, as long as the restrictions are of non-discriminatory character.[165]

Despite the fact that international human rights law does not explicitly introduce an obligation to the states to provide publicly financed teaching in minority languages, the Aland Islands minority rights regime is far ahead of that in linguistic and educational rights protection. It is quite evident that there is no conflict in the minority rights protection regime in the Aland Islands and the international human rights treaties and their provisions. Even with respect to Finnish-speakers in the Aland Islands, the case lacks a problematic, as they are entitled to use their own language when dealing with public authorities according to the Section 37 of the

164 Horn, *supra* note 152, pp. 167–169.
165 Öst, *supra* note 153, p. 83.

Autonomy Act, communicate in their language in public and private.[166] Even so, the creation of more reasonable opportunities to use the Finnish language and enjoy Finnish culture that follow from the general development of Western European societies toward multiculturalism, were suggested by Hannikainen as recommended measures to ensure that there would be no feelings of unease created by exclusive domination of Swedish language in the Aland Islands.[167] Nonetheless, this recommendation does not belittle the exemplary nature of the Aland Islands minority protection regime that deserves recognition as one of the most developed in international legal practice to date.

Concluding remarks

This part of chapter has analyzed the main points of the Aland Islands precedent from the international legal point of view. The Aland Islands precedent is a success case of the League of Nations and an example of a reasonable approach of states willing to settle the argument peacefully and where the kin-state (Sweden) has chosen not to use an aggressive approach, even in light of concerns for its kin in the Aland Islands. On the other hand, Finland has accepted the limitations to its sovereignty over the Aland Islands in order to protect the culture and language of the minority in these territories and to allow a broad self-governance in the autonomy.

The Aland Islands precedent also features the perfect example of the exercise of internal right of self-determination by the minorities in the sovereign state, without threatening its territorial integrity, and the development of the autonomy in the best possible way for the minority in question. The islands enjoy not only a very broad self-governance that communicates very closely with the state on wide range of matters but also manifests a unique demilitarized and neutralized status that provides security guarantees not only for the population of the Aland Islands, but generally, to the overall situation in the Baltic Sea region. Moreover, the Aland Islands feature one of the most developed minority rights protection regimes in the world.

The precedent of the Aland Islands and its autonomy find a lot of resemblance with the Nagorno-Karabakh Conflict, which also features the questions of self-determination, interests of a kin-state, a territory with strategic and geopolitical importance, a compact national (ethnic) minority and its

166 Horn, *supra* note 152, pp. 181–182.
167 Hannikainen, *supra* note 154, p. 65.

interests and security, as well as questions of autonomy and possible resolution through self-governance and protection of minority rights. Thus, this study will proceed with a comparative analysis of the Nagorno-Karabakh Conflict situation and the Aland Islands precedent in order to find common features (as well as principal differences) between an unresolved conflict and a successfully developing precedent, in order to discern if there are possibilities to use these successful experiences to solve the conflict between Armenia and Azerbaijan.

3 Nagorno-Karabakh and Aland Islands cases compared

When considering the possibility of comparing the two cases of Nagorno-Karabakh and the Aland Islands it is important to draw the boundaries in which the comparison will be embedded. These boundaries will provide a framework that will suit the purpose of this book in the best possible way. Without these boundaries there is a risk of spillover into the matters of history, politics and sociology that are undoubtedly very important for conflict studies but irrelevant to the scope of this particular analysis.

The Aland Islands precedent and the Nagorno-Karabakh Conflict have a pronounced number of similarities that lie in: a) the historical context, b) positions of the conflicting parties toward the conflict issues, c) similarity of arguments from the parties to the conflict, d) involvement of third states as greater powers, e) legal arguments and their validity and f) other matters that will be discussed in this chapter of the book. At the same time, there are differences that cannot be overlooked during the comparative analysis that will be provided here. Both situations have differences in geographical location, time period in history, states involved and even different international legal frameworks that have been in place. One is a success story that is in the post-conflict stage and still developing as a model for autonomy and conflict resolution. The other case is still in the conflict stage with no resolution visible as of yet. It is thus important to differentiate between various features of these cases that can and should be compared, to reflect them in this international legal analysis and to differentiate between those particular features that are incomparable due to the objective factors, such as the relevance of the geographic status – the Aland Islands constitute an exclave, while Nagorno-Karabakh is an enclave.

Nonetheless, it is both similarities and differences of these cases that will be evaluated here in order to draw appropriate conclusions on the possibility of using best practices of the Aland Islands to facilitate the resolution of the Nagorno-Karabakh Conflict in accordance with international law. It is thus paramount not to confuse the real political situation on the ground

DOI: 10.4324/9780429353437-3

and international legal norms that are applicable to both situations. While both are interconnected, this book is not going to research and analyze the political background of the resolution and development of the Aland Islands precedent and the peace process in the Nagorno-Karabakh Conflict. Rather the comparison will be based on the legal aspects of the resolution of the Aland Islands question and the subsequent development of the autonomy and corresponding legal aspects of the Nagorno-Karabakh Conflict.

Furthermore, this section of the book will avoid as much as possible the dangers of going too deep into the legal theory, prioritizing instead an approach that puts the primary sources first and then proceeds further down the line only if such sources do not satisfy the necessity for the analysis or are simply nonexistent. This will ensure that the comparative legal analysis will not be drifting away from reality too much and will not have a negative effect on conclusions and jeopardize the outcomes of the analysis.

One other goal this comparative legal analysis will try to achieve is to keep the integrity of the norms of international law that are applicable to both cases and avoid their distortion. While making a comparison between two distinctly similar cases, it is sometimes even unconsciously tempting to bend the arguments toward the desired outcome that facilitates an easier and "cleaner" answer to the posed questions. Thorough comparative legal analysis, however, reduces this risk to a minimum, as it is essential for the interpretation of both national laws and international norms, and even facilitates the possibility to apply these norms correctly in the future.[168] Moreover, when analyzing the applicability of certain features of the Aland Islands precedent to the Nagorno-Karabakh Conflict, comparative legal analysis will be decisive for the proper argumentation on the applicability of each feature.

For the purposes of this chapter, the comparative analysis will concentrate on specific areas of the Aland Islands precedent and the Nagorno-Karabakh Conflict. The starting position of the analysis will be the comparison of these cases in a historico-legal retrospective that will identify the similarities and differences of conflict situations in each case and provide the context for analysis of concrete issues that are common to both cases. One such issue revolves around questions of self-determination under the international law raised in both cases. The chapter will examine how the questions of self-determination have defined the context of both cases and whether it is possible to talk about concrete similarities or the unique differences that

168 Danny Pieters, *Functions of Comparative Law and Practical Methodology of Comparing. Or How the Goal Determines the Road!*, in Syllabus Research Master in Law, Leuven-Tilburg, 2009, http://bit.ly/2k5e9iI, pp. 6–7.

make these cases comparable/incomparable in terms of the right of peoples to self-determination.

On the other hand, the chapter will examine the minority issues in each situation in order to see where concerns for minority rights have been satisfied from the point of view of international law and where these rights have suffered in terms of their violation and inapplicability. The basis of these concerns in both cases is of particular interest, as it can help to identify if the working guarantees of the Aland Islands precedent can be applied to the resolution of the Nagorno-Karabakh Conflict, taking into account that the resolution of the conflict will ultimately be based on international law and subsequent specific guarantees, no matter what the agreement of the conflicting parties will be in the end.

At the same time, the roles of the state-parties to the conflict, international organizations and third states involved in the resolution of the Nagorno-Karabakh Conflict and the historic solution of the Aland Islands question will be compared and examined accordingly, in order to draw parallels between the behaviors of these actors. Such comparison will enable the author to suggest adjustments to policies and behavior under international law for the actors engaged in the resolution of the Nagorno-Karabakh Conflict in order to facilitate such a resolution. While concentrating on the comparative legal analysis, this part of the chapter will attempt to draw a clear picture of the possible applicability of the Aland Islands precedent to the Nagorno-Karabakh Conflict's resolution.

Comparative analysis in the historico-legal perspective

When it comes to the comparison of the cases of the Aland Islands and Nagorno-Karabakh, the first thing that comes to mind in the historical retrospective is that both territories that have become the objects of an international dispute carry a strategic importance, not only to the states that were engaged in the conflict over exercise of sovereignty, but to the third parties as well. For example, the strategic location of the Aland Islands in the Baltic Sea and their importance for the security situation there explains the stark interest that not only Sweden and Finland but other states like the UK, France, Germany and Russia have expressed throughout history, which was discussed earlier. Moreover, it is generally understood that after the 1856 demilitarized and then neutralized status of the Aland Islands, the islands became a part of a wider European legal and peace order.[169] When it comes to Nagorno-Karabakh, this piece of land was historically located in the

169 Vesa, *supra* note 87, pp. 37, 51.

region that was a point of nexus of three empires – Ottoman, Persian and Russian (modern Turkey, Iran and Russia, respectively).[170] In this unique situation, it is quite clear that Nagorno-Karabakh was of particular importance not only for Azerbaijanis and Armenians but was also included in the overall strategic framework perceived by the larger state actors.

Another particular issue that is common for both cases is that until 1917–1918 both the Aland Islands and Nagorno-Karabakh were sovereign parts of Imperial Russia. With the independence of Finland in 1917 and Azerbaijan in 1918, this sovereignty came to an end, although in the case of Azerbaijan it was a short-lived experience. By 1921, Azerbaijan, along with Nagorno-Karabakh, was reincorporated into Russia under Soviet rule. Still, it is necessary to point out that the first questions of sovereignty over territories of the Aland Islands and Nagorno-Karabakh were prompted by the fall of Imperial Russia and its retraction from the territorial gains it once had achieved. While the Aland Islands question found its resolution in 1921, some scholars suggest that the problem with the Nagorno-Karabakh question was that due to the internal policies of the Soviet Union, it failed to solve the issue by the creation of an autonomous region of NKAO (The Nagorno-Karabakh Autonomous Oblast), and instead suppressed and conserved it, only to see it reemerge in 1988 as a conflict.[171]

At the same time, both cases feature a minority that lives on the territory that is an object of the conflict. In the Aland Islands, the Swedish population has been a constant factor through most of the islands' history with a very static demography that was never affected considerably by other ethnic groups.[172] On the other hand, the Nagorno-Karabakh region was historically populated by both Armenians and Azerbaijanis. Here the demographic situation changed considerably several times, and Armenians became a majority in this region and a minority within Azerbaijan, surrounded by predominantly Azerbaijani-populated territories during the period of the Soviet Union. The increase of the Armenian population in Nagorno-Karabakh is seen in the 19th century due to Russian policies in the post-war situation with the Persian Empire.[173] Although there is a difference between the historical formation and status of the minorities in both of these cases, this does not affect their legal status as a national (ethnic) minority or their standing from the point of view of international law.

170 Cornell, *supra* note 3, pp. 4–6.
171 Ibid., pp. 8–13.
172 *See* Vesa, *supra* note 87, p. 37; Hannikainen, *supra* note 154, p. 14; Potier, *supra* note 5, p. 56.
173 Cornell, *supra* note 3, p. 5.

Moreover, it is important to identify historical parallels in order to compare the minority situation in both cases and argue for the implementation of an appropriate regime if needed. It is possible that the differences in the formation of the minority and demographic situation are the result of the differences in geographical status of territories in both cases.

While the Aland Islands are an archipelago and an exclave of Finland's mainland,[174] Nagorno-Karabakh is, on the other hand, an enclave in the territory of Azerbaijan.[175] Islands are, of course, less prone to demographic changes of population both in terms of their "exclusion" from the mainland's dynamics of internal migrations and from the point of view of general geographic isolation. In the case of a mountainous enclave historically lying on the crossroads of different trade routes, such as Nagorno-Karabakh, the situation is different. Arguably, only the mountainous character of the region allowed it to preserve regional ethnic majority for some time through history, until the creation of autonomy there during the Soviet Union.

That brings another commonality between the cases into historical perspective. Both territories in question gained autonomy in the early 1920s. However, the status and development of those autonomies have been quite different. In the case of the Aland Islands, the final resolution of the conflict came from the efforts of an international organization and support of the international community. The autonomy proved its status through faithful implementation by Finland and even developed and expanded its status and protection of the Swedish minority. In the case of Nagorno-Karabakh, the autonomy status was granted by the decision of the Soviet Union and the Communist Party and was subject to the same system of governance that was implemented in the USSR. This system of governance will be discussed further in this chapter in order to show the difference between proclaimed autonomy of Nagorno-Karabakh, that was not implemented in practice, and an exemplary one of the Aland Islands.

It is only logical that with the minority factor so important in the resolution of both conflicts, the questions of self-determination have been historically very important in both cases. As it can be seen from the argument so far, the right of peoples to self-determination is not applicable to Nagorno-Karabakh or to the Aland Islands. However, it is important to make a comparison between the origins of these questions in both cases to

174 Potier, *supra* note 5, p. 56; Vesa, *supra* note 87, p. 37.

175 Nicholas W. Miller, 'Nagorno-Karabakh: A War without Peace', in Kristen Eichensehr and W. Michael Reisman (eds.), *Stopping Wars and Making Peace: Studies in International Intervention*, Martin Nijhoff Publishers, 2009, p. 43.

identify the possibility of application of internal self-determination available to minorities.

Minority rights and protection issues

The fate of the Swedish minority living on the islands was always in the center of the Aland Islands question. The concern of the population of the islands with their rights and security was quite evident at the time of the resolution of the question by the League of Nations.[176] That genuine concern was one of the factors that prompted Finland to grant the islands an autonomy in the first place. Moreover, that concern was at the core of the guarantees that were provided by the international community (through the League of Nations) to the islands.[177] The development of the minority rights in the Aland Islands autonomy was discussed earlier, but it is also important to make a comparison and determine whether and in what part the international law on minority rights and protection that is applicable to the Aland Islands is also applicable to the Nagorno-Karabakh.

To begin the analysis with the applicable law that was developing at the same time with the autonomy of the Aland Islands, it seems logical to start with the definition of the minority as a subject of protection in international law. Although there is no internationally agreed and binding definition of the minorities,[178] there are still widely recognized criteria that can be found in the international legal doctrine that allows for the categorization of a specific group as a minority as such. Most comprehensive such criteria are based on the definition of minorities by the Special Rapporteur Capotorti to the UN Sub-Commission on Prevention of Discrimination and Protection of Minorities of 1977[179] and its reiteration in the Recommendation 1201 (1993) of the Parliamentary Assembly of the Council of Europe. Those criteria include: 1) numerical criterion, that the subject group should be numerically inferior to the rest of the population; 2) criterion of non-dominance, that maintains that the subject group should not be in the position of hegemony; 3) criterion of distinctiveness, that requires that the subject group and its members be different by ethnicity, religion or language from the rest of the population; 4) criterion of cohesiveness, requires that the members of the group should explicitly or implicitly show a sense of

176 Barros, *supra* note 89, pp. 69, 230–231.

177 Suksi, *supra* note 103, pp. 64–65.

178 OHCHR, *Minority Rights: International Standards and Guidance for Implementation*, UN, 2010, www.ohchr.org/Documents/Publications/MinorityRights_en.pdf, p. 2.

179 Ibid.

solidarity directed toward preservation of their culture, traditions, religion or language; 5) criterion of affiliation, that requires ties to exist between the subject group and the country in which they reside.[180]

While the Swedish-speaking population of the Aland Islands in no doubt fits these criteria[181] (as also discussed in Chapter 2 and thus enjoys the rights and protection through international law, Finnish law and its autonomous status, the definition in question can be applied to the Armenians in Nagorno-Karabakh as well. Today, the highest estimations of the population of Nagorno-Karabakh put it at 153,000 people.[182] While the current population of Azerbaijan is estimated at approximately 9.94 million people,[183] the numerical criterion is clearly satisfied. Armenians differ from Azerbaijanis ethnically, religiously and linguistically, but are quite close culturally, sharing a lot of common features in music, arts and cuisine. Armenians were never a hegemonic group or a minority in power in Azerbaijan and always had close ties with Azerbaijan as a state, being its residents and citizens since the establishment of the Soviet Union. On the other hand, the fact of the preservation of language, religion and culture and organized movement for self-determination is a clear sign that Armenians of Nagorno-Karabakh satisfy the criterion of cohesiveness as well. Thus, it is clear that the minority status is applicable to both cases that are being compared.

Minorities in international law enjoy quite a wide protection based on the number of international treaties and documents. For the Swedish-speaking population of Aland Islands the protection of their language and culture was essential and the same can be said for the Armenian minority in Nagorno-Karabakh,[184] which is very concerned with the same issues defining them as a minority and a part of a nation living outside the country with identical ethnic ties. There are provisions that cover the protection of language and culture through linguistic and educational rights that are rooted in the famous Article 27 of the Covenant on Civil and Political Rights. However, its provisions are quite declaratory and very general. They are clarified somewhat only by the general comments of the Human Rights Committee. At the same time, the 1992 UN Declaration on the Rights of Persons belonging to the National or Ethnic, Religious and Linguistic

180 Horn, *supra* note 152, pp. 152–153.

181 Ibid.

182 Slomanson, *supra* note 79, p. 31.

183 World Bank Data, *Azerbaijan*, 2018, https://data.worldbank.org/country/azerbaijan.

184 Carol Migdalovitz, *Armenia-Azerbaijan Conflict*, CRS Issue Brief for Congress, Air University, August 8, 2003, www.au.af.mil/au/awc/awcgate/crs/ib92109.pdf, p. 3.

Minorities builds upon the scope of Article 27. In Article 4(3), it imposes an obligation on the states to take appropriate measures to ensure that minorities can have the possibility to learn their language or have instruction in their mother tongue.[185] Moreover, the Human Rights Committee in its General Comment No. 23 on Article 27 of the Covenant on Civil and Political Rights in 1994, has stated:

> The right of individuals belonging to a linguistic minority to use their language among themselves, in private or in public, is distinct from other language rights protected under the Covenant. In particular, it should be distinguished from the general right to freedom of expression protected under Article 19. The latter right is available to all persons, irrespective of whether they belong to minorities or not.[186]

Thus, the Committee made the distinguished character of the linguistic protection of the minorities clear, making it a special protection for any such group.

Moreover, the 1989 Convention on the Rights of the Child has a provision in Article 30 that clearly states that any child belonging to ethnic, religious or linguistic minority shall not be denied the right to use his or her own language,[187] making it obligatory for the states to allow children the use of minority language. This protection extends even further if we consider it in conjunction with the provisions of the 1960 UNESCO Convention against Discrimination in Education. Article 1(1) of this international treaty has clearly defined the notion of discrimination in education:

> 1. For the purposes of this Convention, the term "discrimination" includes any distinction, exclusion, limitation or preference which, being based on race, colour, sex, language, religion, political or other opinion, national or social origin, economic condition or birth, has the purpose or effect of nullifying or impairing equality of treatment in education and in particular: (a) Of depriving any person or group of persons of access to education of any type or at any level; (b) Of limiting any person or group of persons to education of an inferior

185 United Nations General Assembly, *UN Declaration on the Rights of Persons belonging to the National or Ethnic, Religious and Linguistic Minorities*, 1992, A/RES/47/135, http://bit.ly/1hyvqWL, art. 4(3).

186 *CCPR General Comment No. 23: Article 27 (Rights of Minorities)*, 8 April 1994, CCPR/C/21/Rev.1/Add.5, www.refworld.org/docid/453883fc0.html, art. 5.3.

187 UN General Assembly, *Convention on the Rights of the Child*, A/RES/44/25, 1989, www.ohchr.org/EN/ProfessionalInterest/Pages/CRC.aspx, art. 30.

> standard; (c) Subject to the provisions of Article 2 of this Convention, of establishing or maintaining separate educational systems or institutions for persons or groups of persons; or (d) Of inflicting on any person or group of persons conditions which are incompatible with the dignity of man.[188]

Thus, the provisions covering the right for education for minorities are also clear. The aforementioned Convention, however, goes further and makes a specific provision in Article 3(d) that does not allow states to make "in any form of assistance granted by the public authorities to educational institutions, any restrictions or preference based solely on the ground that pupils belong to a particular group".[189] This means that minorities are entitled to the same assistance in education as anybody else in the state, while having a right to be educated in their own language.

Nonetheless, it appears that the 1960 UNESCO Convention against Discrimination in Education in the scope of provision of minority rights was more restrictive than the Aland Islands autonomous regime at the time. In its Article 5(1)(c), it states: "It is essential to recognize the right of members of national minorities to carry on their own educational activities, including the maintenance of schools."[190] This seems like a great provision that provides clear education rights for minorities to maintain their own schools, but it was heavily criticized in scholarship for being very conditional. It appears that being more of a freedom than the right, this provision is limited by the requirement that it does not prevent members of a minority group from understanding the culture and language of the community they are a part of as a whole, does not negatively affect the national sovereignty, does not lower the education standard for the minorities compared to the overall population and even that attendance of minority schools should not be mandated. Due to these conditions, Finland faced a lot of challenges when actually ratifying this international treaty.[191] Despite that fact, Finland was still able to become a part of the treaty, and the treaty itself generally provides a basic protection for minorities and their education rights that can be applied to both cases under consideration in this book.

188 UNESCO, *Convention against Discrimination in Education*, 14 December 1960, www.unesco.org/education/pdf/DISCRI_E.PDF, art. 1.

189 Ibid., art. 3(d).

190 Ibid., art. 5(1)(c).

191 Horn, *supra* note 152, pp. 172–174; Hannikainen, *supra* note 154, pp. 41–49.

Both Azerbaijan and Finland are a part of the Council of Europe, and that is why it is also important to take into account this framework of minority protection. The European Convention on Human Rights and its Protocols gives limited overall protection in terms of educational rights, that, nonetheless, is still important. Article 2 of the First Protocol to the Convention solidifies the right of everyone to education, and if read in conjunction with Article 14 of the European Convention on Human Rights itself that bans discrimination,[192] it can be safely said that these provisions ensure the rights of minorities for education. Scholars who have analyzed the compatibility of the Aland Islands regime with the provisions of this Convention, drawing analogies with the Belgian Linguistics case, come to the conclusion that the Aland Islands regime does not violate the norms set out by the European Convention on Human Rights.[193]

At the same time, it is clear that it is the 1992 European Charter for Regional or Minority Languages that has the most solid provisions concerning the linguistic and educational rights of minorities. Article 7(1), detailing the objectives and principles of the minority protection in a broader sense, sets forth a powerful set of provisions and states:

> In respect of regional or minority languages, within the territories in which such languages are used and according to the situation of each language, the Parties shall base their policies, legislation and practice on the following objectives and principles: (a) the recognition of the regional or minority languages as an expression of cultural wealth; (b) the respect of the geographical area of each regional or minority language in order to ensure that existing or new administrative divisions do not constitute an obstacle to the promotion of the regional or minority language in question; (c) the need for resolute action to promote regional or minority languages in order to safeguard them; (d) the facilitation and/or encouragement of the use of regional or minority languages, in speech and writing, in public and private life; (e) the maintenance and development of links, in the fields covered by this Charter, between groups using a regional or minority language and other groups in the State employing a language used in identical or similar form, as well as the establishment of cultural relations with other groups in the State using different languages; (f) the provision of

192 Council of Europe, *European Convention for the Protection of Human Rights and Fundamental Freedoms, as amended by Protocols Nos. 11 and 14*, 4 November 1950, ETS 5, www.echr.coe.int/Documents/Convention_ENG.pdf.

193 Horn, *supra* note 152, pp. 174–177; Hannikainen, *supra* note 154, pp. 36–39.

> appropriate forms and means for the teaching and study of regional or minority languages at all appropriate stages; (g) the provision of facilities enabling non-speakers of a regional or minority language living in the area where it is used to learn it if they so desire; (h) the promotion of study and research on regional or minority languages at universities or equivalent institutions; (i) the promotion of appropriate types of transnational exchanges, in the fields covered by this Charter, for regional or minority languages used in identical or similar form in two or more States.[194]

Noting this exceptional set of principles, it is quite important to stress sections (a) and (f) of this article, which are most important for the cases compared, in terms of value of the minority language and the ability to teach and study them in all stages of education. That said, it has to be pointed out that Finland already ratified the Convention in 1994, while Azerbaijan signed it in 2001 but has not ratified as of the time of writing of this book.[195]

As can be seen, international law covering minority protection has a wide range of norms that guarantee linguistic, educational and cultural rights and are applicable in both the cases of the Aland Islands and Nagorno-Karabakh. No less important, however, are the civil and political rights that bring us to the discussion of issues of self-determination in the same context.

Self-determination issues

The issues of self-determination are embedded deeply in both Aland Islands and Nagorno-Karabakh cases. However, as it was discussed earlier, the right of peoples to self-determination in broader sense is not applicable either to the Aland Islands question or to the Nagorno-Karabakh Conflict, because the populations of both of these territories constitute national (ethnic) minorities who cannot claim the external right to self-determination. It is thus logical that the issues that will be discussed and compared here will focus on the internal self-determination that is applicable in the case of minorities.

194 Council of Europe, *European Charter for Regional or Minority Languages*, 5 November 1992, ETS 148, www.coe.int/en/web/conventions/full-list/-/conventions/rms/0900001680695175, art. 7(1).

195 Council of Europe, *Chart of Signatures and Ratifications of Treaty 148*, Status as of 03/10/2017, www.coe.int/en/web/conventions/full-list/-/conventions/treaty/148/signatures.

During the resolution of the conflict over the Aland Islands, the League of Nations faced the question of internal self-determination. Markku Suksi, citing the Commission of Jurists appointed by the League of Nations, points out that the principle of self-determination

> must 'be brought into line with that of the protection of minorities; both have common object – to assure to some national Group the maintenance and free development of its social, ethnical or religious characteristics.' The Commission suggested that … 'Under such circumstances, a solution in nature of a compromise, based on an extensive grant of liberty to minorities, may appear necessary according to international legal conception and may even be dictated by the interests of peace'.[196]

This position of the Commission shows that it was already deliberating over the question of how minorities can benefit from the principle of self-determination. As it can be seen from the quotation, in the opinion of the Commission, the aim of self-determination in case of minorities is preservation and maintenance of their culture (society), ethnicity or religion. Moreover, granting extensive liberties may be necessary according to international law and simple interests of peace. These views have solidified since 1921 into the concept of internal self-determination as we know it today.

Interestingly, the Commission of Jurists pondered these questions during the general discourse that was quite prominent at the time. The principle of self-determination was a part of the then-popular Fourteen Points of U.S. President Woodrow Wilson, and Wilson himself was a staunch promoter of the principle.[197] Even the founder of the Soviet Union, Vladimir Ilyich Ulyanov (Lenin) was a great supporter of the principle of self-determination and Wilson's ideas in this regard.[198] Lenin's works on the principle featured his opinion that ethnic or national groups were able to demand autonomy while remaining part of the greater state structure.[199] The historical context, thus, created an opportunity for the consideration of these ideas as early as the beginning of the 1920s.

Nevertheless, the development of the principle of self-determination continued in a different direction. After the two world wars, the international community was more worried about the fate of "peoples" and

196 Suksi, *supra* note 103, p. 64.
197 Vesa, *supra* note 87, p. 43.
198 Crisan, *supra* note 56, p. 113.
199 Potier, *supra* note 5, p. 22.

especially "colonial peoples". The applicability of self-determination to these categories, rather than to minorities remained higher on the agenda for a long time. The right of peoples to self-determination had been included in the UN Charter's Article 1, which reads:

> The Purposes of the United Nations are: 1. To maintain international peace and security, and to that end: to take effective collective measures for the prevention and removal of threats to the peace, and for the suppression of acts of aggression or other breaches of the peace, and to bring about by peaceful means, and in conformity with the principles of justice and international law, adjustment or settlement of international disputes or situations which might lead to a breach of the peace; 2. To develop friendly relations among nations based on respect for the principle of equal rights and self-determination of peoples, and to take other appropriate measures to strengthen universal peace; 3. To achieve international co-operation in solving international problems of an economic, social, cultural, or humanitarian character, and in promoting and encouraging respect for human rights and for fundamental freedoms for all without distinction as to race, sex, language, or religion; and 4. To be a centre for harmonizing the actions of nations in the attainment of these common ends.[200]

However, even then it was included in the UN Charter in the meaning of the right to self-government of the peoples and not the right of secession.[201]

In line with that, the right of peoples to self-determination was included in the two UN Covenants, on Civil and Political Rights and on Economic, Social and Cultural Rights that were adopted in 1966. In their identical Article 1 they state:

> 1. All peoples have the right of self-determination. By virtue of that right they freely determine their political status and freely pursue their economic, social and cultural development. 2. All peoples may, for their own ends, freely dispose of their natural wealth and resources without prejudice to any obligations arising out of international economic co-operation, based upon the principle of mutual benefit, and international law. In no case may a people be deprived of its own means of subsistence. 3. The States Parties to the present Covenant, including those having responsibility for the administration of Non-Self-Governing

200 *UN Charter*, www.un.org/en/sections/un-charter/chapter-i/index.html, art. 1.
201 United Nations Conference on International Organization, Vol. VI, p. 298.

> and Trust Territories, shall promote the realization of the right of self-determination, and shall respect that right, in conformity with the provisions of the Charter of the United Nations.[202]

The focus of the international community on "peoples" and the principle of self-determination started to expand to cover minorities as well, largely after the decolonization process was practically over. The provisions of the Helsinki Final Act, discussed earlier in this book, show that the international community was coming back to the ideas that minorities should also benefit from self-determination in order to preserve their ethnicity, culture, religion and language and be able to exercise civil and political rights in the form of self-government that should not interfere with the territorial integrity of the state they live in.

Moreover, leading international legal scholarship has taken the stance on self-determination as serving first of all an internal function. Cassese, analyzing these questions as they relate to the Covenant on Civil and Political Rights, writes that self-determination

> presupposes freedom of opinion and expression (Article 19), the right of peaceful assembly (Article 21), the freedom of association (Article 22), the right to vote (Article 25(b)), and more generally the right to take part in the conduct of public affairs, directly or through freely chosen representatives (Article 25(a)). Whenever these rights are recognized for individuals, the people as a whole enjoy the right of internal (political) self-determination; whenever these rights are trampled upon, the right of the people to self-determination is infringed.[203]

This is a very important conclusion that clearly shows that internal self-determination is possible with the proper application of civil and political rights for minorities. As the Aland Islands example of autonomy clearly shows, this idea is as close to reality as international law can be. The importance of such "political" self-determination is also applicable to the case of Nagorno-Karabakh and explains the necessity behind the struggle of its minority, even if ill-directed.

202 UN General Assembly, *International Covenant on Civil and Political Rights*, General Assembly resolution 2200A (XXI), 1966, http://bit.ly/1Oq5JFt, art. 1; UN General Assembly, *International Covenant on Economic, Social and Cultural Rights*, General Assembly resolution 2200A (XXI), 1966, http://bit.ly/J1E1V3, art. 1.

203 Patrick Thornberry, 'The Principle of Self-determination', in Vaughan Lowe and Colin Warbrick (eds.), *The United Nations and the Principles of International Law: Essays in Memory of Michael Akehurst*, New York: Routledge, 2002, p. 192.

At the same time, it is necessary to stress that as the decolonization process came to an end, the internal aspect of self-determination was ultimately linked to the autonomy as a viable intra-state solution. While this may be true, it is not possible to agree with the oversimplification that internal self-determination should be narrowed down to the selection of a desired system of government.[204] Internal self-determination instead allows minorities to construct the symbiosis with the state that ensures them the most comfortable opportunities for development and maintenance of their culture, language and religion. On the other hand, it is true that states are wary even of the autonomy arrangements in cases of internal self-determination. As the Venice Commission noted:

> States seem in fact to be afraid that the right to have appropriate local or autonomous authorities, combined with the right to transfrontier contacts … , may promote secessionist tendencies. Even those States which, while adhering to the principle of unitarity have granted a large degree of regional autonomy hesitate to accept binding international instruments on the right of minorities to a certain autonomy.[205]

Despite that fact, the states like Finland, that have embraced the idea of adopting high-level minority standards and are not afraid to follow-up on minority obligations, enjoy more prosperous and rewarding systems of autonomous rule than do states that are cautious of the international legal arrangements.

States also fear for the representatives of the majority group in the minority-dominated area. As on one hand, decentralization of the state in terms of smaller political units with substantial autonomy will lead to greater protection from the abuse coming from the central government's authorities, it can lessen the protection of other groups or majority representatives living with the minority.[206] For example, while Armenians were a majority in the former Nagorno-Karabakh Autonomous Oblast, Azerbaijanis constituted a minority there. During the war, they were expelled from Nagorno-Karabakh and adjacent territories,[207] and that greatly affected the peacemaking process in negative terms, resulting in the

204 Michla Pomerance, *Self-Determination in Law and Practice: The New Doctrine in the United Nations*, The Hague and London: Martin Nijhoff, 1982, p. 37.

205 Potier, *supra* note 5, pp. 66–67.

206 Dinah Shelton, 'Subsidiary, Democracy and Human Rights', in D. Gomien (ed.), *Broadening the Frontiers of Human Rights*, Oslo: Scandinavian University Press, 1993, p. 54.

207 Miller, *supra* note 175, p. 54.

tougher position of Azerbaijan on the issue. Nonetheless, such fears for the majority's well-being should not prevent the state from accepting the internal self-determination of minorities in the form of autonomy. With the right approach it is possible to solve this issue. As the Aland Islands example shows, the Finnish-speaking population of the islands is quite comfortable and does not require special protection in terms of minority rights.[208]

Nonetheless, if internal self-determination is possible through autonomy in the form of consensus between the majority and the minority, it is still not clear if the autonomy is a 'right' in itself. It has to be pointed out that most probably it is not. Potier strongly disagrees with Heintze that any "right" of autonomy comes from customary law in the form of its frequent appearance, stating that while constitutional law may have a principle that is historically on the path of ascension into the customary international law, it is still too early to place it on the same scale as principles of international law, as there is no treaty law confirming the right to an autonomy or even a confirmed state practice. Potier still acknowledges that it may be a "future" for the autonomy, as states become increasingly more under internal pressures and may be prompted to resort to the "right" of autonomy, even if as a last resort measure.[209]

Indeed, such observations speak in favor of autonomy as a solution for internal self-determination and allow us to draw even more parallels in the cases of the Aland Islands and Nagorno-Karabakh. In the end, it is really hard to disagree with the observation of former UN Secretary General Boutros Boutros-Ghali in 1992 in the Agenda for Peace when he stated:

> The United Nations has not closed its door. Yet if every ethnic, religious or linguistic group claimed statehood, there would be no limit to fragmentation, and peace, security and economic well-being for all would become ever more difficult to achieve.[210]

With that in mind, it has to be pointed out that the attitudes and will of the states and international organizations toward the possible solutions that can bring lasting peace in matters of internal self-determination are also very important.

208 Horn, *supra* note 152, p. 182.
209 Potier, *supra* note 5, pp. 68–69.
210 UN General Assembly, *Agenda for Peace*, A/47/277, S/24111, 1992, www.un-documents.net/a47-277.htm, para. 17.

Roles of the state-parties, international organizations and third states involved in the settlement of the Aland Islands question and the Nagorno-Karabakh Conflict

The Aland Islands question had found its resolution as far back as 1921 and it remains a long-lasting solution to the conflict since the beginning of the 20th century, while the Nagorno-Karabakh Conflict has been plaguing the peace and security in the region of South Caucasus for more than a quarter of a century. With great similarities between the issues from the point of view of international law (as it can be seen from the earlier discussion) that lie at the core of both of these cases, why are their respective fates so different?

Just like international law is heavily dependent on the will of the states,[211] so is the maintenance of peace and security and conflict resolution. Today, the readiness and willingness of states-parties to the conflict to find a resolution through peaceful means is crucial for the maintenance of global peace and security, and yet, such willingness can be ensured by the international community, through specific mechanisms that are embedded into the UN Charter and vested into the UN bodies charged with the conflict resolution and maintenance of peace. It is even more striking, that during previous times of conflict between Sweden and Finland, such mechanisms did not exist and nonetheless the Aland Islands question found its resolution, while the Nagorno-Karabakh Conflict is still an issue.

In this sense, it is important to take a look at what measures were taken by Sweden and Finland as parties to the conflict and compare them with steps taken by Armenia and Azerbaijan, while examining the role of international organizations and third parties involved in each of these cases and how they affected the peace process in the Aland Islands and in Nagorno-Karabakh.

In the first stages of the conflict between Sweden and Finland, the former was supportive of the population of the Aland Islands in their desire for unification with Sweden. At the same time, it was not in the interests of Sweden to count Finland as a non-friendly state at first. At the time of the Paris Peace Conference, Sweden's position was simplified to a proposed plebiscite in the Aland Islands that would decide its fate, and it was, of course, known to Sweden how this vote was going to play out. The Finnish position, on the other hand, was against any plebiscite in the Aland Islands and held that these territories were historically, geographically and

211 Rüdiger Wolfrum, *Max Planck Encyclopedia of Public International Law*, 2006, http://bit.ly/2kpzSCa, para. 13.

economically a part of Finland; Finland also held that the Swedish-speaking population of the islands was a part of a whole Swedish-speaking minority of Finland and not a separate entity. While parties to the conflict and other European states involved were not able to find a solution during the Paris Peace Conference, Britain and France played a key role in a decision to leave the solution to the newly created international organization – the League of Nations – to which the question was finally referred by Britain.[212] In 1920, while pending the resolution from the League of Nations, the conflict between Sweden and Finland was escalating. In order, to prevent the secessionist movements in the Aland Islands, Finland extended the islands an autonomy, that was, however, rejected by the population of the islands because the matter was not discussed with them and was seen as an imposed measure rather than a negotiated one.[213]

Quite differently, when the conflict began to simmer between Armenia and Azerbaijan on the brink of the dissolution of the Soviet Union, Armenia was already present militarily in Nagorno-Karabakh. It similarly supported the plebiscite that, unlike in the Aland Islands, took place in the Nagorno-Karabakh in 1991, but the Azerbaijani minority in the region was not able to participate in it, as it was already mostly expelled from the territory of the enclave, while the rest have boycotted the referendum. Interestingly, the Armenians of Nagorno-Karabakh who were similarly expressing their will for the unification with Armenia, chose to vote for independence in the referendum in hopes of using the dissolution of Soviet Union as a pathway to independence and the consequent unification with Armenia. The reaction of Azerbaijan to the referendum was the abolition of the autonomy in the Nagorno-Karabakh region. After the dissolution of the Soviet Union, when Armenia and Azerbaijan became independent states, the full-blown war broke out between them over the territory of Nagorno-Karabakh.[214] The matter then became a responsibility of the UN Security Council. As most of the initial events were happening still inside of the dying USSR, there were no third parties that could intervene or refer Armenia and Azerbaijan to the mediation of the international organization. However, the difference between the behavior of Sweden and Finland, and that of Armenia and Azerbaijan is striking when one looks at how Armenia chose to resort to military action so early in the conflict and how Azerbaijan eliminated the autonomy in the Nagorno-Karabakh, instead of trying to do its best to engage its minority.

212 Vesa, *supra* note 87, pp. 43–45.
213 Barros, *supra* note 89, p. 216; Jansson, *supra* note 94, p. 3.
214 Cornell, *supra* note 3, pp. 22–29.

In both cases that are under consideration, international organizations played important parts. In the case of the Aland Islands, the League of Nations was a mediator that was actively working on the resolution of the conflict. In the Nagorno-Karabakh Conflict during the first stages of war between Armenia and Azerbaijan, the United Nations (through its body charged with the maintenance of peace and security – the Security Council) was a primary international organization seized on the matter of the conflict. The two organizations operated in very different time periods and global political environments and functioned on very different levels. However, it is still possible to draw parallels in their conflict resolution activities and see what they have done for the resolution of the conflict and what means and instruments were available to them at the time. It has to be kept in mind that the League of Nations was a first-in-kind international organization charged with maintenance of global peace. It was mandated with settling international disputes through negotiation and arbitration. However, unlike the UN, it lacked the mechanisms of enforcement of its decisions. The UN, on the other hand, has such mechanisms available to the organization under the UN Charter.

For the League of Nations, the Aland Islands question was one of its first major challenges. Nonetheless, it managed to solve the issue and make both Sweden and Finland agree to a binding decision. It has to be pointed out that Finland's *de facto* sovereignty over the Aland Islands was confirmed as *de jure* by the Council of the League of Nations decision.[215] As it was discussed earlier, the League of Nations was very thorough in its investigation of the question and based its decision on the opinions of two commissions. The first commission determined that the issue was not a domestic one for Finland and that the League of Nations was an appropriate authority to solve the issue. The second commission, examining the merits of the case, found in favor of the sovereignty of Finland on conditions of autonomy, minority protection and demilitarization of the Aland Islands. The implementation of the decision of the Council of the League of Nations was supported by Britain and France, which had permanent seats on the Council, and the objections of Sweden were not sustained in this matter.[216] It is remarkable how the League of Nations, using a collective will of states that constituted its Council, was able to persuade the parties to the conflict to agree to a binding decision and to fulfill the subsequent obligations.

215 Hannikainen, *supra* note 119, p. 57.
216 Vesa, *supra* note 87, pp. 45–47.

On the other hand, in the Nagorno-Karabakh Conflict, the UN Security Council was dealing with the issue while the war was still raging between Armenia and Azerbaijan. In 1993, while Armenia was progressing in the occupation of the territories of Azerbaijan, the UN Security Council adopted four resolutions that demanded cessation of such actions from the Armenian side and withdrawal of Armenia from the occupied territories.[217] Armenia, surprisingly, to this day has not fulfilled the requirements set out by the UN Security Council in the resolutions. It is even more surprising considering the fact that unlike the League of Nations, the UN Security Council has means and mechanisms to enforce its resolutions under Chapter VII of the UN Charter. However, in the case of Nagorno-Karabakh, the UN Security Council until this day has not adopted any resolutions under Articles 41 or 42 of the UN Charter to impose sanctions of economical or military character on Armenia to ensure the compliance of this state with the UN Security Council resolutions. Thus, the 1993 resolutions on the Nagorno-Karabakh Conflict have not been implemented for almost 25 years. Moreover, what happened is that the UN chose to transfer its responsibility for dealing with the conflict to a regional organization (OSCE). Unlike the League of Nations, the UN chose not to be involved so deeply in the resolution of the Nagorno-Karabakh Conflict. It limited its own role to the resolutions of the Security Council, which did not even define Armenia as an aggressor.[218] Such an approach contributed to the prolongation of the conflict.

During the resolution of the conflict over the Aland Islands, third parties and interested states were very active on the diplomatic side, helping the resolution to succeed with diplomatic efforts and mediation. The UK and France, the U.S. and even Norway contributed to the fair and just resolution of the conflict over the Aland Islands.[219] While surely acting in their respective interests, they nonetheless were able to produce a positive result in the form of a solution to the question. On the other hand, the UN Security Council was unable to move forward with the resolution of the Nagorno-Karabakh Conflict and chose to abandon its responsibility in favor of a regional organization – the OSCE. This organization has created a format for the resolution of the conflict – the so-called "Minsk Group". While initially this format consisted of multiple states, by 1997 only three states (France, Russia and the U.S.) have managed to solidify and centralize the resolution process by the institution of permanent co-chairs of the

217 Krüger, *supra* note 28, p. 106.
218 Cornell, *supra* note 3, p. 116.
219 Barros, *supra* note 89, pp. 216–333.

"Minsk Group".[220] Until today, the co-chairs have been unable to deliver a resolution of the conflict. This format itself was criticized as ineffective, and the co-chair states are more concerned with upholding the *status quo* of the conflict rather than with its resolution.[221] Hence, in the Nagorno-Karabakh Conflict, the attitudes and will of third parties and interested states took a different direction, as mentioned earlier. Preservation of the situation as a lesser evil seems to be fitting into the framework of the negative reasoning that France, Russia and the U.S. chose to adopt in the resolution of the Nagorno-Karabakh Conflict. The importance of these states and their will (or lack of it) to implement international law should not be underestimated.

Barros rightly mentions the role of the states and international organizations in the conclusions to his study on the resolution of the Aland Islands question:

> [When] great power cooperation is not forthcoming, decisive action against any aggressor has proved impossible. The collective security feature of international organization pivots on the willingness of the great powers to act in concert for the benefit of [the] international community. Naturally, political tension of competition between or among the states in this grouping, either within or without the organization, is reflected in their ability or inability to cooperate for the universal goals for which the organization is striving and in which their unique position in the gallery of states has given them a privileged role.[222]

Indeed, the will of states to cooperate within and outside the international organization has allowed states to achieve a resolution of the conflict over the Aland Islands. Quite logically, it is the lack of will of states and their failure to cooperate in different formats and organizations that complicates the final and just resolution of the Nagorno-Karabakh Conflict in the framework of international law.

Concluding remarks

This part of the book made a comparative analysis between the cases of the Aland Islands and Nagorno-Karabakh in an attempt to point out the

220 Cornell, *supra* note 3, pp. 116–117.
221 Rossi, *supra* note 3, pp. 67–69.
222 Barros, *supra* note 89, p. 335.

common features and distinct dissimilarities between them. Such an analysis is also important in terms of applicability of the Aland Islands precedent to the Nagorno-Karabakh Conflict. At the same time, a comparative analysis took into account the differences in historical and legal perspective that are applicable to both cases, making comparisons without prejudice to the points that simply cannot be compared due to the aforementioned differences.

It is indeed an interesting fact that since the 19th century and up to 1917, both the Aland Islands and Nagorno-Karabakh were under the sovereignty of the same state of Imperial Russia. The major issues of both conflicts have many similarities. Both cases under comparison are territorial conflicts with the minority population that has a kin-state. In both cases, the resolution depends on the well-being of the minority in question. While the right of peoples to self-determination does not apply in a broader sense, the internal self-determination based on the minority rights and respect of territorial integrity of the state can be a feasible solution for the Nagorno-Karabakh Conflict as adopted from the experiences of the Aland Islands. It is also important to see how the minority rights issues are close in both cases and that the ability to ensure these rights in the autonomous framework is a crucial point for both of these cases.

It has also been quite evident that the differences between these two cases lie primarily in the dimension of the will of states (both engaged in the conflict and third parties) and attitudes of international organizations toward the resolution of both conflicts. While in the case of the Aland Islands the states in question and international organization were on a positive track to resolution, the situation is quite the opposite in the case of the Nagorno-Karabakh Conflict.

Thus, provided that the will of the states and commitment of international organizations to a just and final resolution of the Nagorno-Karabakh Conflict can be ensured, it is quite evident that the similarities between the two cases allow for the consideration of the Aland Islands precedent as a model for the resolution of the conflict over Nagorno-Karabakh. The implementation of such a solution and the applicability of the aforementioned model will be analyzed further later in this book.

4 Aland Islands precedent as a model for the resolution of the Nagorno-Karabakh Conflict

As has been previously discussed, there are great similarities between the problematic issues in the already resolved situation in the Aland Islands and the unresolved Nagorno-Karabakh Conflict. Thus, logic suggests that it is indeed important to ponder the possibility of using the best practices of the former precedent to solve the latter conflict. Following this line of thinking, in this chapter an attempt will be made to show, first, that the Aland Islands precedent can be considered a model for the conflict resolution from the perspective of international law. Second, the chapter will follow up with the analysis of previous notable attempts of comparison of the Aland Islands precedent with the Nagorno-Karabakh Conflict, in order to be aware of the previous experiences and studies and take them into proper consideration. Third, the chapter will attempt to outline the resolution of the Nagorno-Karabakh Conflict within the framework of international law using the Aland Islands precedent and its most important elements as a model and a base. Finally, the chapter will provide general recommendations on the resolution of the Nagorno-Karabakh Conflict based on the summarized research and analysis.

While following the aforementioned outline, this chapter will try to avoid the political nuances of the conflict resolution as much as possible, trying to keep the analysis and the discussion in the framework of public international law. Minor references to historical and political contexts will be made only in the larger context of legal arguments and inasmuch as the need for their support. While the author of this book is acutely aware of the importance of the political and historical arguments in the overall context of the resolution of the Nagorno-Karabakh Conflict, for the purposes of this research, the book's focus is bound to the international law issues, leaving other dimensions secondary to this subject. Moreover, the humanitarian side of the issue will be taken out of the discussion as well. Such complex issues as refugees and IDPs, international criminal justice and prosecution, reparations leading from the armed conflict and aggression, etc., will not

DOI: 10.4324/9780429353437-4

be discussed here, as they fall outside the scope of this book, although they are also of remarkable importance to conflict resolution.

In line with the scope of this book, these aforementioned issues are recognized as important for the post-conflict situation, whenever the Nagorno-Karabakh Conflict is solved in accordance with norms of public international law. Thus, the author leaves these important and sensitive issues to the parties to deal with after the resolution of the situation itself. Such an approach seems more rational and in line with the substance of international law, devoid of the emotions that (being part of human nature) can sometimes be harmful to its proper application. It then seems logical that such emotional topics as refugees and war crimes may be discussed and resolved separately or (better) after the resolution of the main issues plaguing the territorial conflict.

On the other hand, despite the fact that similarities between two cases under consideration do exist, it is still important to discuss what actually makes the Aland Islands precedent so attractive and appropriate to be considered as a model for the resolution of the Nagorno-Karabakh Conflict.

The Aland Islands precedent: a model for the conflict resolution?

While discussing the value of the Aland Islands precedent, it seems appropriate to start with an explanation of the term "model" that will be used in the context of this chapter. It has to be pointed out, that "model" as a term is not favored in scholarly works, even by the authors who are actively working on the promotion of the Aland Islands as a precedent for the conflict resolution. Sia Spiliopoulou Åkermark argues that the term "Åland Example" is better suited for the needs of conflict resolution. She states:

> [T]he Åland Example, aspires to give insights in the components and preconditions that made the peaceful solution of the dispute between Finland and Sweden possible in 1921 and to understand and explain why this regime has survived for more than 90 years (of autonomy and neutralisation) and more than 150 years of demilitarisation. The idea of a 'model', by contrast, implied the faint hope and possibility that the regime may be transported and used, more or less in its entirety, in other ethno-political and territorial disputes.[223]

223 Sia Spiliopoulou Åkermark, 'Introduction', in Sia Spiliopoulou Åkermark (ed.), *The Åland Example and Its Components – Relevance for International Conflict Resolution*, Mariehamn: Åland Islands Peace Institute, 2011, p. 8.

While it is hard to disagree with this explanation, it still has to be pointed out that the term model used in this study does not imply even the remote possibility of a copy/paste solution of the Nagorno-Karabakh Conflict using the regime in the Aland Islands. Rather, the term "model" used here lies in the middle between the definitions of "Åland Example" and "model" provided by Åkermark.

The model of the Aland Islands precedent for the purposes of this book is a combination of its selected features (elements) that can be used as a set of carefully tailored measures taken in the resolution of the Nagorno-Karabakh Conflict. These elements can be selected based on the comparative analysis provided earlier in this book. Thus, after the discussion of what makes the Aland Islands precedent a "model" for the purposes of this book, it will be possible to select the appropriate elements and attempt their application to the Nagorno-Karabakh Conflict.

One of the things that should be considered about the Aland Islands precedent is that, despite its success, it is still a serious challenge to the idea and even to the paradigm of state sovereignty. Autonomies around the world are widespread, but that does not make them the norm but rather an exception to the concept of state sovereignty and thus problematic. In this line of thinking, Åkermark provides three components of what she calls an "Åland Example": 1) demilitarization and neutralization of the Aland Islands through the series of treaties; 2) self-governance of the Aland Islands as a legal system; 3) the protection of language and culture on the Aland Islands since 1921 up to the modern levels of protection.[224] All of these issues have been discussed earlier in this book. All of them have parallels with the situation in Nagorno-Karabakh.

Moreover, it is quite well understood by many scholars that the longevity of the Aland Islands precedent makes it possible to talk about it as a model formed naturally through the passage of sufficient time. Krister Wahlback even suggests that such a long-lasting solution became an international model for conflict resolution.[225] Such views expressed come from the ponderings of scholars on the longevity and successful development of the autonomy in the Aland Islands.

Markku Suksi, for example, also mentions that the self-governing regime of the Aland Islands is sometimes counted globally as the oldest existing

224 Ibid., p. 9.

225 Pertti Joenniemi, 'Åland in the New Europe: A Case of Post-Sovereign Political Life', in Lauri Hannikainen and Frank Horn (eds.), *Autonomy and Demilitarisation in International Law: The Åland Islands in a Changing Europe*, Kluwer Law International, 2007, p. 12.

autonomy arrangement and is thus considered exemplary.[226] He also notes this in his longevity argument, when discussing the differences between autonomy and federalism. He explains that the Aland Islands are not a federally organized part of Finland in any way. In an excellent explanation, Suksi states:

> [A] territorial autonomy involves a singular entity in what otherwise would be a unitary state or a federal state, so that the entity introduces an asymmetrical feature in the state through a transfer of exclusive law-making powers on the basis of provisions, which often are of a special nature and defined in such a manner that the central state level remains with the residual powers, while the sub-state level relies on enumerated powers, at the same time as the state level contains no institutional representation of the sub-state entity.

Such structure differs substantially from the federal one, based usually on the symmetry of treatment of sub-entities as well as their institutional representation in the legislative body of the state. While Suksi acknowledges that there is a small deviation from this setting in the case of the autonomy of the Aland Islands, it is an insubstantial one and cannot change the categorization of the islands as a territorial autonomy.[227] He refers, of course, to the separation of powers between the Finnish Parliament and the Legislative Assembly in the Aland Islands, which were discussed earlier in the book.

Moreover, such facts as: 1) constitutional entrenchment of the autonomous arrangement in Finland; 2) the need to obtain the consent of the legislative power in the autonomy to make any changes into the autonomous arrangement; 3) the status of the amendments to the autonomous regime equalized with the status of the amendments to the Constitution of the state of Finland; 4) responsibility of Finland under international law to uphold and guarantee the autonomy of the Aland Islands, give even more credibility to the arguments on the robustness and longevity of the Aland Islands precedent.[228] The special rights that have been granted to the population of the Aland Islands, apart from the autonomous arrangement and directly by the national legislation, include, for example, exemption from the conscription to military service, the special seat in the national

226 Markku Suksi, 'Explaining the Robustness and Longevity of the Åland Example in Comparison with Other Autonomy Solutions', *International Journal on Minority and Group Rights*, Volume 20, No. 1, 2013, p. 51.

227 Ibid., pp. 56–57.

228 Ibid., pp. 58–60.

parliament, right of domicile in the form of regional citizenship that grants access to additional rights, entrepreneurship rights.[229] Such developments in the autonomy done through negotiations and developments on a national level are ultimately favoring the longevity of the autonomous arrangement in the islands as well.

On the other hand, coming into the field of mixed internal and external factors, Åkermark suggests, based on the research by Yash Ghai, that there are five clusters of crucial factors that influence the success or failure of the autonomy: 1) higher chances of the success of the autonomy in times of regime change or a wider re-shuffle in the state and/or region in question; 2) heavy dependency on the nature of the dispute that can itself harm any meaningful and long-term solution; 3) democratic nature of the host state; 4) different roles of the external actors; 5) institutional design, its attractiveness and change over time.[230] What these clusters of factors actually explain is a peculiar phenomenon, such as the increased relevance of autonomous arrangements in the postcolonial world, on the background of a very restrictive right of peoples to self-determination, and continuously disputed questions of sovereignty and limitations on the sovereignty of states. The less contested sovereignty, thus, leads to a less problematic autonomy-based solution. Moreover, it seems that Ghai's arguments include the increased likelihood of the success of the autonomy-based solution, given the democratic nature of the host state. Democratic compromises, thus, can make the development and integration of the autonomous solution less problematic, while such compromises are features of the states with established democratic history. Also true is that while the position of the great powers is undeniably important, it has to be taken into account that the success of the autonomous arrangement presupposes that the external actor of such kind will not become a direct party to the conflict. In line with the arguments of Suksi, the factors of institutional design and its entrenchment into the legislation of the host state have to be reconsidered with time and developed in the manner tailored to the current needs of the autonomy, and that is where the goodwill of the host state is most important.

Unto Vesa is of a similar opinion that, for some time already, different cases have been compared with the Aland Islands precedent, especially where the matters of self-determination may be applicable. The precedent, thus, has been referred to as a model and a source of lessons to be learned, especially when it comes to the demilitarization issues. Asking a valid

229 Ibid., p. 66.
230 Åkermark, *supra* note 223, pp. 18–23.

question of what kind of lessons can be learned from the precedent, Vesa very accurately points out:

> The most valuable and relevant lessons may be at the level of principles: full protection of minority rights and sufficient autonomy taking into account the historical, local and cultural conditions. [Also], the accommodation of competing interests, demilitarization, autonomy, the positive role of third parties as mediators, the inquiry method as the basis of exploring the factual merits, as well as the responsiveness towards each other's interests and values are essential elements in the resolution of territorial disputes.[231]

Indeed, it is hard to find better referencing to the elements of the Aland Islands precedent. Autonomy and minority rights, coupled with security and positive role of third parties and external actors, should ensure success, provided that the parties to the conflict themselves are willing and ready to solve the issue peacefully through the autonomous arrangement.

On the other hand, paying more attention to the details as such, Elisabeth Naucler argues that though the Aland Islands precedent is usually presented as an example and a success story, it is still not completely free from shortcomings. However, even these shortcomings are important to be studied in finding a workable model for other cases. Such shortcomings, she argues, are, for example, the status of the Finnish-speaking population in the Aland Islands that are still considered a majority and the reluctance of Finland to work in the direction of minority within minority protection. On the other hand, the ascension of Finland to the EU, has been problematic beacuse of the autonomous status of Aland Islands that have such strong constitutional standing that they may have been left out of the EU if they so wished. Even today, after the ascension of Finland to the EU has prompted some changes in the autonomous arrangement of Aland Islands, in Naucler's view, these changes are still not satisfactory. Despite the mentioned shortcomings, she also suggests that the importance of demilitarization and neutralization of the islands should not be overlooked, as it is a first-in-kind used as a confidence-building measure in the area where no armed conflict has been actively taking place. Moreover, she argues that Finland should promote the knowledge of the positive example of the Aland Islands to the conflicting parties globally and even as a "brand".[232]

231 Vesa, *supra* note 87, p. 57.

232 Elisabeth Naucler, 'The Åland Solution Applied', in Sia Spiliopoulou Åkermark (ed.), *The Åland Example and Its Components – Relevance for International Conflict Resolution*, Mariehamn: Åland Islands Peace Institute, 2011, pp. 156–158.

Indeed, it is hard to disagree with Naucler that there are no perfect examples and nothing flawless, especially when it comes to such complex topics as state governance and autonomy. However, as she rightly points out, even the shortcomings are worth consideration and careful study. These exceptions, in particular, only support the argument that the Aland Islands precedent can be considered a model for conflict resolution, provided that its elements are carefully studied and their application to the resolution of any given conflict is well researched and tailored to the realities of the conflict in question. In this sense, not surprisingly, the Nagorno-Karabakh Conflict, as well as some other similar situations, have been brought up in the context of conflict resolution using the Aland Islands precedent as a model in international legal scholarship.

Previous reflections on the applicability of the Aland Islands precedent to the resolution of the Nagorno-Karabakh Conflict in international legal scholarship

The similarities between the situations in the Aland Islands and Nagorno-Karabakh have not gone unnoticed in international legal scholarship. However, it has to be pointed out that none of the scholars that have pondered the idea of using the Aland Islands precedent as a model for the resolution of the Nagorno-Karabakh Conflict have gone so far as to make a comprehensive comparative analysis, which has been attempted by this book. Nonetheless, their ideas and reflections on this matter deserve to be mentioned and discussed here, as they are the basis of the arguments and counterarguments that will be used in this book to show how the Aland Islands precedent can be used for the resolution of the Nagorno-Karabakh Conflict.

One of the early and very limited comparisons was done by Tim Potier in his work on conflicts in Nagorno-Karabakh, South Ossetia and Abkhazia. While discussing the theory and practice of the autonomy in general, Potier singles out the Aland Islands as an autonomous, demilitarized and unilingual Swedish province of Finland.[233] When further discussing the process of political solution in the Nagorno-Karabakh Conflict, he raises the Aland Islands precedent once again, stressing the following:

> The Bosnian version is unacceptable to Azerbaijan. They will not accept the principle of 'two states created in the framework of one state'. Instead, they prefer a level of autonomy similar to that enjoyed

233 Potier, *supra* note 5, p. 56.

> by the Aland Islands or Tatarstan. These, at least, are acceptable to Yerevan, which views the 'state of affairs' in these autonomies as being considerably different to the situation in the South Caucasus, let alone Karabakh.[234]

As can be seen, in the view of Potier, the Aland Islands as a case was at least considered by both Armenia and Azerbaijan, and was not utterly rejected, which brings hope that there can be common ground and understanding here.

In his work, Potier comes up with a set of recommendations for the resolution of the Nagorno-Karabakh Conflict. Further in his work, he discusses his recommendations and shows the logic and reasoning of his proposals in the form of commentaries. Among other cases, he comments on the Aland Islands precedent and discusses what he thought was applicable and not applicable from this case to the Nagorno-Karabakh Conflict. For example, Potier states that the highest aspiration in the case of Nagorno-Karabakh would be its demilitarization. However, Potier is skeptical of whether it will be possible to achieve that in some feasible way and in a reasonable time. Instead, he believes that neutrality may be much easier to implement. Surprisingly, Potier is also skeptical of adaptation of a self-governing regime from the Aland Islands, as he believes that the Aland Islands are not in fact a self-governing territory because Finland maintains a lot of powers in foreign policy, civil and criminal law, justice, customs and monetary services, even despite extensive budgetary powers granted to the islands. Potier further explains:

> [M]y recommendations do not envisage any form of legislative representation for Karabakh in the *Milli Majlis* (Parliament of Azerbaijan). Most certainly Karabakh would never, under any circumstances, agree to the Republic of Azerbaijan 'appointing' a Governor to 'watch over' the republic.

Nonetheless, Potier acknowledges that there are many points of potential commonality. One feasible feature, in his opinion, would be the introduction of "regional citizenship" using the same principles as in the case of the Aland Islands. As long as this citizenship will not be parallel to the citizenship of Azerbaijan and there will be no language requirement, Potier thinks, this may be a great feature to have in the resolution of Karabakh. The regional citizenship, in his point of view, should not target real estate

234 Ibid., p. 86.

and business opportunities, like in the Aland Islands, but in the case of Karabakh, it should be a prerequisite for election rights (voting and running for the office). For refugees and IDPs though, there should not be any time limit for the resettlement and claims on regional citizenship.[235]

There seem to be two main problems with Potier's argumentation on the subject. First, he tries to take the Aland Islands precedent as a whole and fit it straight to the Nagorno-Karabakh Conflict, getting rid of the elements he deems unnecessary in the process. It would be much more appropriate to study the elements of the Aland Islands precedent separately and then argue their applicability, based on substantial legal research. Second is the lack of research to support his arguments on the choice of some features and rejection of others. A very clear example is that he dismisses the institution of the Governor, stating that it will not be accepted by Armenians of Nagorno-Karabakh. Potier misses the fact that the position of the Governor is not one of a "ruler" from the central government (even symbolically). The Governor's role is a facilitation of the dialogue between the autonomy and the central state and thus is a very important role in communication, as it was discussed previously in this book. Nonetheless, Potier's attempt of comparison is important for further deliberations.

Swedish diplomats on the highest level have also been involved in the resolution process of the Nagorno-Karabakh Conflict and mentioned parallels with the Aland Islands precedent. Former Swedish Foreign Minister Jan Eliasson, who acted as a Chairman of the Minsk Conference of OSCE on Nagorno-Karabakh, shed some light on comparisons drawn between the Aland Islands and Nagorno-Karabakh in an interview with the Aland Islands Peace Institute. Eliasson mentioned that delegations to the Aland Islands from Armenia and Azerbaijan have been making visits even before he stepped in as a Chairman of the Minsk Conference. While there was a clear interest shown in the Aland Islands as an example of conflict resolution, Eliasson believes that the parties were always worried about giving up their negotiating positions and ultimately tied the Aland Islands precedent with the issue of the future status of Nagorno-Karabakh, concentrating on the autonomy aspect.[236] Sadly, but due to the limitations of the diplomatic process, instead of concentrating on the situation as a whole, the Aland Islands precedent was narrowed down to only one of its main ele-

235 Ibid., pp. 200–201.

236 Heidi Öst, 'Åland and the Nagorno-Karabakh Negotiations in the South Caucasus', in Sia Spiliopoulou Åkermark (ed.), *The Åland Example and Its Components – Relevance for International Conflict Resolution*, Mariehamn: Åland Islands Peace Institute, 2011, pp. 163–164.

ments – self-governance in form of an autonomy v. the status of Nagorno-Karabakh. Fortunately, international legal analysis provides freedom from such constraints.

Heidi Öst in her analysis identifies a very interesting point. She cites common analytical responses from the representatives of the parties to the violent conflict in Nagorno-Karabakh when confronted with the Aland Islands precedent as an example. Most of these responses dismiss the precedent as a solution found between two countries from "developed civilization", state that Finland has "purchased" the Alands Islands, assume that there were no violence and bloodshed in the case of the Aland Islands, etc.[237] Such statements are, of course, far from being true. As has been indicated earlier in this book, the people of the Aland Islands have lived through considerable violence during the course of their history and some of it was connected to the conflict between Sweden and Finland. The solution itself was found by international mediation and not a "purchase". Moreover, tensions between the two countries were very high during the whole process and perhaps were not so different from the situation in Nagorno-Karabakh in the beginning of the 1990s.

What is interesting is that Öst confirms in her analysis that all of the main features of the Aland Islands precedent have been discussed in South Caucasus, at one point or another, with respect to the Nagorno-Karabakh Conflict. In her point of view, however, the most important and immediate element of the solution should be demilitarization and its relevance to the prevention of new war in the Nagorno-Karabakh region. The agreement on the demilitarized zone is, thus, seen as a great basis on which further confidence-building measures can be built to ensure the peaceful resolution of the conflict.[238] It is hard to disagree with such an assessment. Instead of concentrating on the factor of self-governance and what rights and protection the minority will get in the process, it seems more logical to, first, find a solution for the question of how to take the arms out of the equation – that then will be followed up by other elements of the solution in line with the Aland Islands precedent. One thing should be different, though, when considering the demilitarized zone and applying the "demilitarization" as a feature of the Aland Islands precedent. There is a need for such demilitarization to be a regional solution (based on the agreement with other major states in the region) rather than a bilateral agreement between two parties. This needs to be done in order to ensure the goodwill of external actors, just as had happened in the Baltic Sea a century ago.

237 Ibid., p. 166.
238 Ibid., p. 167.

As Unto Vesa fairly states: "[L]essons learnt from one case have to be applied to the specific features and conditions of other cases, be it in Nagorno-Karabakh or Tanzania."[239] Such specific features and conditions will always be the case. That, however, is not a sufficient argument to disregard the use of positive experiences of conflict resolution and miss an opportunity to implement them elsewhere. Using the lessons learned from the solid arguments as well as mistakes made by the previous analysis of the applicability of the Aland Islands precedent to the Nagorno-Karabakh Conflict and comparative research provided in this study, it is thus possible to proceed with a presentation of the vision of implementation of the Aland Islands precedent into possible resolution of the Nagorno-Karabakh Conflict within the framework and in accordance with international law.

Implementation of the elements of the Aland Islands precedent into the resolution of the Nagorno-Karabakh Conflict

As the previous analysis shows, the three most important elements of the Aland Islands precedent can be used as a basis for the model of resolution of the Nagorno-Karabakh Conflict. These three elements applied to the conflict in question can be generally outlined as: 1) demilitarization and neutralization of the territory of Nagorno-Karabakh; 2) self-governance as an autonomous region within territorial integrity of Azerbaijan; 3) comprehensive protection of minority rights of the Armenian population living in the region of Nagorno-Karabakh as a majority.

In order to provide a realistic assessment for the matter, it is important to note that the resolution of the conflict in the form of the implementation of these three elements can only be possible if both parties to the conflict, third states (such as France, Russia and the U.S.) and international organizations engaged in the resolution of the conflict will accept international law as a primary basis for the resolution of the Nagorno-Karabakh Conflict. Such an acceptance will direct the will of the states toward the solution in positive, non-violent key, based on restraint, compromise and acceptance of the norms of international law. Moreover, strict adherence to the agreements reached after the resolution is also extremely important, as shown by the positive example of Finland.

Provided that the aforementioned conditions are fulfilled, the first element of the resolution can be applied in the form of demilitarization and neutralization of Nagorno-Karabakh. Presently, the situation on the

239 Vesa, *supra* note 87, p. 57.

ground in the region of the Nagorno-Karabakh Conflict can be described by the so-called line of contact (LoC) between the armed forces of Armenia and Azerbaijan. This is an extremely shaky and uneven line that separates two armies and is frequented by the violations of cease-fire agreement concluded between the parties in 1994.[240] It is quite evident that in such a tense situation the resolution of the conflict can profit, first and foremost, from demilitarization, to ensure that there will be no arms "talking" in Nagorno-Karabakh while the peace process is underway. It is, thus, important to take a look at what demilitarization and neutralization actually mean.

Definitions of the aforementioned terms that were provided by Rosas have been discussed earlier in this book in relation to the regime in the Aland Islands. However, for the purposes of proper implementation of demilitarization and neutralization as an element of the resolution of the Nagorno-Karabakh Conflict it is important to elaborate a little more on this topic. In international law, the terms of demilitarized and neutralized zones describe a specific legal status related to the territory in question. At the same time, there are no universally or generally accepted definitions of these terms. Most of the definitions are considered *ad hoc* in state practice, in each particular case. With that in mind, it may be useful for the purposes of this book to adopt a working definition for the aforementioned terms based on the research done by Christer Ahlström, who studied a number of *ad hoc* cases from the practice of the European states. Ahlström defines a demilitarized zone as: "a legal regime which sets forth a qualitative or quantitative reduction of military potential in a defined geographic area". He explains that *ratione materiae* of a demilitarized zone is a qualitative or quantitative reduction of military potential in the defined area that can be implemented in form of obligations to disarm or not to acquire certain weapon systems (qualitative) or in limiting number of troops or weapon systems (quantitative). As to the neutralized zones, Ahlström explains that they

> are generally formulated in a very succinct manner, stipulating that the geographical area in question may never be used for the conduct of military operations during wartime situations. The legal status of a neutralised zone thus differs from that of a demilitarised zone in that it is intended to apply during a wartime situation. The *ratione materiae*

240 Bayramov, *supra* note 14, p. 117.

of neutralized zone is to prohibit the conduct of military operations in a defined geographic area.[241]

As can be seen from this discussion, Ahlström's definitions are more narrow than those of Rosas in terms of application. Of course, Ahlström's basis for definitions were different *ad hoc* cases, while Rosas concentrated on the regime of the Aland Islands. Nonetheless, both of these definitions are useful, and here is why. It seems more realistic to apply the demilitarization and neutralization regime in Nagorno-Karabakh in two stages. In the first stage, it is absolutely crucial to bring the two states (Armenia and Azerbaijan) to an agreement on the demilitarized zone on the whole territory affected by the Nagorno-Karabakh Conflict using the more narrow definition provided by Ahlström, with a condition that the qualitative and quantitative reduction in the demilitarized zone will proceed until the absolute minimum that is possible to achieve is reached. That will lead to better possibilities to continue the implementation of the resolution in the peaceful manner.

In the second stage, another agreement in the form of a multilateral treaty should be concluded in line with the more restrictive definition of Rosas, that the territory of Nagorno-Karabakh will be fully demilitarized with no military installations or troops present there ever, and that its territory will never be used for military purposes during an armed conflict. The demilitarization and neutralization regime can be adopted from the positive experiences of the Aland Islands and extended, if the parties to the agreement will wish for and agree on more provisions or guarantees. The treaty should be multilateral and include, apart from Armenia and Azerbaijan, at a very least co-chair states of Minsk Group, namely France, Russia and the U.S., and preferably even more regional states, namely, Georgia, Iran and Turkey. The state-parties to such a treaty, apart from Armenia and Azerbaijan, will serve as guarantors of the demilitarization and neutralization regime in Nagorno-Karabakh. The interests of the regional states in the stability and security of the region will presuppose their dedication to the guarantees for such a regime. Adopting the provision from the experience of the Aland Islands that such demilitarization and neutralization regime should stay in power despite any changes in the regional *status quo* or under whose authority (sovereignty) Nagorno-Karabakh will be, should

241 Christer Ahlström, 'Demilitarised and Neutralised Zones in a European Perspective', in Lauri Hannikainen and Frank Horn (eds.), *Autonomy and Demilitarisation in International Law: The Åland Islands in a Changing Europe*, Kluwer Law International, 2007, pp. 41–43.

only strengthen the power of such an agreement. With demilitarized and neutralized Nagorno-Karabakh, security issues of the conflict should be resolved enough to pave the way to the questions of the autonomy and its functioning within the territory of Nagorno-Karabakh.

For the autonomy to function properly in Nagorno-Karabakh, it is important that it would be entrenched on the constitutional and the highest legislative level possible in Azerbaijan. It would be possible to achieve such an entrenchment by implementing the fundamental guarantees based on the corresponding legal experience of the Aland Islands precedent. One of the most important features in this experience is, of course, the Autonomy Act and its evolution with the development of autonomy. As we are already past the 20th century, it is logical to base the recommendations on the latest Autonomy Act of 1991.

As it was discussed earlier, the Autonomy Act contains provisions and norms on the substance of the self-governance and the autonomy of the Aland Islands. It sets the general framework and limits of the autonomy and provides fundamental provisions on the organization of the legislative and executive bodies in the autonomy, explains the right to domicile (also referred to as a form of regional citizenship in the doctrine), provides for the division of powers between the autonomy and the state and the settling of disputes between them and covers economic and tax relations. A very important feature is that this Act was adopted by the parliament of Finland with the approval of the Legislative Assembly of the Aland Islands.[242] The same legislative act should be adopted by Azerbaijan in order to clearly set the fundamental provisions for the autonomy of Nagorno-Karabakh. This Act should be negotiated with the legislative body that can be elected in the autonomy for the first time through temporary voting procedures. Such a body can then participate in the organized joint commission with the legislative representation of the parliament of Azerbaijan to draft the legislative act together, which in the end could be accepted by the parliament in Azerbaijan as well as the legislative body in Nagorno-Karabakh as a founding document of the autonomy. As the experience of the Aland Islands shows, it is not enough to bestow the law of autonomy from top to bottom by the state; the autonomous solution should be negotiated.

Moreover, based on the experience of the Aland Islands precedent, once the act or the law on autonomy is accepted by the parliament of

242 Sten Palmgren, 'The Autonomy of the Åland Islands in the Constitutional Law of Finland', in Lauri Hannikainen and Frank Horn (eds.), *Autonomy and Demilitarisation in International Law: The Åland Islands in a Changing Europe*, Kluwer Law International, 2007, p. 85.

Azerbaijan and a legislative body in Nagorno-Karabakh, any amendments, explanations or limitations to this legislative document (or even its abolition) should be possible only if there is a consent of the legislative body in Nagorno-Karabakh. In the parliament of Azerbaijan it would be logical that such decisions should be made by the qualified majority of 2/3 of the deputies of the parliament, implementing the same requirements as to the adoption of the constitutional laws. Another option is that the act on the autonomy of Nagorno-Karabakh can be elevated to the status of constitutional law as provided by the Constitution of Azerbaijan. For example, such constitutional law is required in order to adopt a new Constitution of the Nakhichevan Autonomous Republic of Azerbaijan.[243]

Such an extraordinarily strong legal protection will allow the autonomous entrenchment to remain intact and in accordance with the will of the population of Nagorno-Karabakh. Moreover, Section 18 of the latest Autonomy Act of the Aland Islands details a very comprehensive list of competences of the legislative body of the Aland Islands. These include: the organization and duties of the Legislative Assembly of the Aland Islands; flag and coat of arms; municipal administration and taxation; public order and security, including fire-fighters and rescuers; building and planning; tenancy and rent regulation, lease of land; environmental protection; healthcare and social care issues; education, culture, sport, youth work, libraries and museums; postal services; farming, forestry, hunting, fishing, roads and canals, creation and penalties for certain offenses and limited trade provisions. Legislative competences of the State are detailed in Section 27 and most notably include jurisdiction over constitutional acts; right of residence and free movement in the country; civil and political rights; foreign relations and trade; family and inheritance law; company law and the accounting; insurance regulations; real property registration and duties; merchant shipping lanes and regulation; nuclear energy (with the consent of the Legislative Assembly for these matters on the territory of the Aland Islands); labor law with some exceptions; criminal law (except certain penalties); administrative deprivation of personal liberty; judiciary and judicial process; citizenship and migration; firearms and ammunition; taxes and dues; monetary policy and other matters.[244]

243 *Constitution of Azerbaijan*, 1995, http://en.president.az/azerbaijan/constitution, art. 134 (VI); Nakhichevan Autonomous Republic is an autonomous exclave within the territorial sovereignty of Azerbaijan.

244 *Act on the Autonomy of Åland* (1991/1144), www.finlex.fi/en/laki/kaannokset/1991/en19911144.pdf, sec. 18 and 27.

Such a consistent and thorough delimitation of competencies is very important, as it keeps any unnecessary disputes to a minimum and helps a state and an autonomy to concentrate on making the system work rather than fight over powers. Of course, the delimitation of powers is a matter of future possible negotiations between central powers in Azerbaijan and authorities in Nagorno-Karabakh, but based on the experience of the Aland Islands, for comprehensive self-governance, such competences as the organization and duties of a legislative body, flag and coat of arms, local administration, taxation, public order and security, building and planning, tenancy and rent regulation, lease of land, healthcare and social care issues, education, culture, sport, youth work, libraries and museums should be ensured to be in the possession of the autonomy and its legislature in any case.

Moreover, the state laws that are adopted by the parliament of Azerbaijan, just like in the case of Finland, should not automatically enter into force on the territory of Nagorno-Karabakh. The legislative body of Nagorno-Karabakh should be able to enact its own laws if it has legislative competence or use template laws, which were previously discussed as a feature of the legislative power in the Aland Islands. It is also important to establish legislative supervision in the autonomy using the institutes that can be based on the Aland Delegation and the Governor of Aland. The names of the institutions can be changed, of course, to something more common to Azerbaijan and Nagorno-Karabakh, but the functioning and the goals can be the same. Most importantly, there is a need to ensure: 1) the functioning of the legislative system, 2) alleviation of contradictions and abolition of collisions in the legislation created by parallel functioning of systems in the autonomy and state; 3) resolution of disputes between the state and the autonomy.

In the case of the Aland Islands, the judiciary is provided by the state and remains in the state competence. This seems logical, as the solidity of the judicial system of the state is important for the rule of law and justice. However, for the Nagorno-Karabakh autonomy, other arrangements can be possible if state and autonomy are willing to negotiate a compromise on these matters. At the same time, the language of the proceedings will be very important in that sense, and brings with it the questions of the minority issues. The role of the judiciary in the guarantees of minority rights and their protection will be very important as well.

Minority rights and their protection are the third important element that should be adopted from the Aland Islands precedent into the resolution of the Nagorno-Karabakh Conflict. During the period since 1921, Nagorno-Karabakh was a part of overall security provided by the state of USSR. On the other hand, its self-governance was possible to the same degree as any other administrative region within the totalitarian rule of the Soviet Union and its Communist Party. Although Nagorno-Karabakh was formally an autonomous region within the territory of the Azerbaijani Soviet Socialist Republic (at the time itself a part of the Soviet Union), the real autonomous self-governance of both Nagorno-Karabakh and Azerbaijan was very limited. This was mostly due to the centralized nature of the USSR's power hierarchy and nature of the communist regime. Nonetheless, Armenians in Nagorno-Karabakh did not suffer from the serious violations of their minority rights under the Soviet Union. They had the possibility of using their own language, maintaining their own culture and receiving education in the Armenian language freely, as these rights were ensured in the USSR on a relatively high level. The transparency of borders between the republics in the Soviet Union made receiving education in the native language very easy and contacts between Armenia and Nagorno-Karabakh borderless.[245]

The problem was that the nexus between the minority rights regime and the real self-governance for the Nagorno-Karabakh Armenians was non-existent. After the collapse of the USSR, the security factor provided by the auspices of the unified country disappeared in the view of the minority, adding even more stress to its large concerns on self-preservation and future development. Thus, the minority rights element is very important, especially in conjunction with security and self-governance, and proves that ensuring only one of these elements is not sufficient for a comprehensive solution based on autonomy and internal self-determination for minorities.

It is important, then, that the minority rights of the Armenian population of Nagorno-Karabakh should be ensured fully. Using the analogy found in the Aland Islands precedent, the language of education, official language of governance, judiciary and other affairs in Nagorno-Karabakh should be Armenian. Moreover, extending the protection for the educational rights of Armenians in Nagorno-Karabakh, Azerbaijan should subsidize all schools in Nagorno-Karabakh regardless of the language of education, while the autonomy of Nagorno-Karabakh should not be obligated to ensure financing of schools where language of education is different from Armenian. That would raise the competitiveness of minority language schools and ensure goodwill of Azerbaijani majority toward

245 Farhad Mehdiyev, Irada Bagirova, Gulshan Pashayeva & Kamal Makili-Aliyev, 'Legal Status of Quasi-autonomies in USSR: Case of Nagorno-Karabakh's Autonomous Oblast', *Caucasus International*, Ankara: Pasifik Ofset Ltd., 2013, Volume 3, No. 1–2, www.academia.edu/5474212/NK_Legal_Status-CI_Vol_3_no_1-2, pp. 143–145.

the autonomy. This difference in approach is based on the fact that unlike in the case of the Aland Islands, the Azerbaijani community of Nagorno-Karabakh is substantively larger than the Finnish-speaking community in the Aland Islands. Thus, to prevent a possibility of preferential treatment from Azerbaijani majority to its own minority in Nagorno-Karabakh, the aforementioned safeguards should be implemented. Moreover, the Armenian language should be elevated to the second official language in Azerbaijan, on a par with Azerbaijani, based on the experience of Finland.

Another important feature of the Aland Islands precedent should also be ensured in Nagorno-Karabakh. Some kind of form of a "regional citizenship", just like the right of domicile in the Aland Islands, should be implemented to protect the Armenian minority in Nagorno-Karabakh. There was a big step taken toward the extension of the autonomy rights in the Aland Islands since 1921. Today, according to the Autonomy Act, the right of domicile is granted only to the residents with adequate knowledge of the Swedish language. Although it took 70 years to implement such a norm in the autonomy of the Aland Islands, the present time allows us to skip the developments and implement the same feature in the autonomous regime right at the beginning of the resolution of the Nagorno-Karabakh Conflict. Ensuring the analogy with the right of domicile would be very important for Nagorno-Karabakh Armenians in terms of the preservation of their autonomous minority regime. While the exact residence time frame for the acquisition of full rights of residency, real estate property rights, trade and entrepreneurship rights and other matters of "regional citizenship" can be defined by the negotiations between Nagorno-Karabakh and the state to better suit the consensus, the language requirement (on the other hand) should be ensured regardless of any other conditions. The only exception in this case should be the returnees to Nagorno-Karabakh, i.e. IDPs from the Azerbaijani community that have lived in its territory before the conflict and constituted around 23 percent of the total population.[246]

The importance of such a requirement was pointed out by Hannikainen in his analysis of the minority rights regime in the Aland Islands:

> [T]he requirement that Finnish-speaking residents in the Aland Islands have an adequate knowledge of Swedish as a condition of the right of domicile has a legitimate aim, is reasonable and there is proportionality between the means employed and the aim sought. The requirement is

246 Caspersen, *supra* note 17, p. 364.

> relatively mild but in the long run it may be an important guarantee for the preservation of the Swedish character of the Aland Islands.[247]

Exactly as in the case of the Aland Islands, the language requirement should be considered mild in case of Nagorno-Karabakh as compared to the positive results it will bring in the long-term relationship between the autonomy and the state.

Furthermore, such issues as broadcasting, media, postal services and other channels of communication should be solved with the same imperative of the preservation of the Armenian minority of Nagorno-Karabakh. These issues play an important role as well, and the treatment of the minority should be preferential in their regard, even if the minority itself has a weaker position or standing in those issues. Adoption and proper implementation of the most comprehensive minority rights treaties (such as the 1992 European Charter for Regional or Minority Languages) by Azerbaijan is highly advisable to ensure that the most comprehensive requirements under international law are satisfied.

As it can be seen from this discussion, proper and thorough implementation of the aforementioned three key elements of the Aland Islands precedent can be a model for the resolution of the Nagorno-Karabakh Conflict. While this may not be an ultimate recipe for the conflict resolution, the stark similarities between the two cases are undeniable. The Aland Islands case has proven itself as a solid precedent that can be used as a model for the resolution of similar conflicts through proper implementation of its elements. Thus, the resolution of the Nagorno-Karabakh Conflict based on the norms and principles of international law can greatly benefit from this precedent.

General recommendations

Based on the comparative international legal analysis of the Aland Islands precedent and the Nagorno-Karabakh Conflict, the general recommendations for the resolution of the latter can be summarized as follows:

1. As the Aland Islands precedent shows, it is only possible to achieve a long-lasting and effective resolution of the territorial conflict provided that there is a positive will of: 1) the states that are parties to the conflict; 2) third states that are interested in the resolution of the conflict, and 3) international organizations that are charged and engaged in

247 Hannikainen, *supra* note 154, p. 56.

the resolution of the conflict in question. Therefore, the critical prerequisite for the resolution of the Nagorno-Karabakh Conflict should be the positive will of (first of all) Armenia and Azerbaijan to achieve peaceful settlement of the conflict, exercise restraint and readiness for the compromise. There should also be a positive will of the third states that are involved in the resolution of the Nagorno-Karabakh Conflict, namely, France, Russia and the U.S., to achieve a just and final settlement of the conflict. These countries should recognize that restoration of peace and security in the area of the conflict is an ultimate interest of all of these states and therefore act accordingly. The international organizations involved in the resolution of the conflict, namely, OSCE and UN, should also deviate from the ineffective policy[248] of maintenance of the *status quo* and the assumption that a relative "no war, no peace" situation is better than nothing and commit to the resolution of the Nagorno-Karabakh Conflict through real mediation rather than using intermediaries in shuttle-diplomacy.

2. In order to settle the conflict, both Armenia and Azerbaijan, as well as France, Russia and the U.S. and the UN and OSCE, should express their dedication to resolving the conflict within the framework of public international law and based on its principles and norms. Using the Aland Islands precedent as an indicator, this can be achieved by the establishment of the mediation body, created *ad hoc* as an international committee, to indicate the solution of the question of Nagorno-Karabakh in accordance with international law under the auspices of an international organization, such as the UN. Such a committee based on the norms of international law and the Aland Islands precedent should make a decision, compulsory to both Armenia and Azerbaijan, that will end the occupation of the territories of Azerbaijan by Armenia and maintain the territory of Nagorno-Karabakh as an integral part of the territory of Azerbaijan on the conditions that Nagorno-Karabakh shall receive a large autonomy and comprehensive minority rights and protection for the Armenian community there. The monitoring body for such an arrangement can be either the UN or the OSCE. The violations of these conditions by Azerbaijan, may result in the aforementioned *ad hoc* body to reevaluate its decision and recognize the right of Nagorno-Karabakh to secession in this particular case. Both Armenia and Azerbaijan should agree to the decision of the committee, recognizing it as legally binding. Both Armenia and Azerbaijan should be obligated by the committee thereafter not to use

248 Rossi, *supra* note 3, p. 70.

force in the resolution of the situation in Nagorno-Karabakh under any circumstances.

3. Based on the Aland Islands precedent, in order to ensure that the resolution of the Nagorno-Karabakh Conflict will bring long-lasting peace in the region, it is recommended to impose the demilitarization and neutralization regime on the whole territory of the Nagorno-Karabakh Conflict (and not only on the territory of Nagorno-Karabakh itself). This demilitarization and neutralization regime should be based on the analogy of the one that is in place for the Aland Islands. It should consist of two levels of international treaties complementing each other. The first level of treaties should be concluded bilaterally between Armenia and Azerbaijan in order to ensure the withdrawal of Armenian troops from the territory of Azerbaijan and step-by-step demilitarization of this territory until the absolute possible minimum. The second level of treaties should consist of a multilateral international agreement (or agreements) between 1) Armenia and Azerbaijan; 2) regional states of Georgia, Iran, Russia and Turkey and 3) international guarantors – France and the U.S. – on complete and ultimate demilitarization and neutralization of the territory of the Nagorno-Karabakh Conflict, guaranteed by the parties to this agreement (or agreements) collectively. The state-parties to such an arrangement can establish a collective organization or an institution to monitor the compliance of the parties with demilitarization and neutralization regime. The longevity of such a regime can be ensured, using the analogy with the Aland Islands, by the provision in the arrangement, that demilitarization and neutralization regime will not depend on which state is exercising the sovereignty over Nagorno-Karabakh and adjacent territories. This will help to establish all the necessary security guarantees to ensure safe environment for the development of the autonomy in Nagorno-Karabakh.
4. Azerbaijan should allow for the highest level of autonomy in Nagorno-Karabakh and entrench its self-governance into the constitutional order and highest levels of legislation in the country. Based on the Aland Islands precedent and the analysis presented earlier, Azerbaijan should ensure that any abolition of the autonomy and all matters delegated to the autonomy by the law and constitutional provisions of the country can only happen with the consent of the autonomy's authorities and an expression of the will of the population of the autonomy. Azerbaijan should create favorable conditions for the development of self-governance in Nagorno-Karabakh and work on the initial autonomous arrangements closely with the elected officials from Nagorno-Karabakh in the atmosphere favorable to the side of the minority and

keeping its best interest in mind. Should Azerbaijan fail to comply with the obligations to establish an autonomy of the highest level for Nagorno-Karabakh, its elected officials should have the right and possibility to raise the matter in the aforementioned *ad hoc* committee, for a reconsideration of the issue.

5. Azerbaijan should adopt all the best practices of modern minority protection. Using the Aland Islands precedent as an example, as well as other best cases of the minority rights protection regimes around the world, it should work closely with elected officials of Nagorno-Karabakh to entrench the minority rights and their protection in the legal framework of the autonomy in Nagorno-Karabakh and in the legislation of Azerbaijan. The main focus should be on the protection of cultural, educational and linguistic rights of the Armenian minority, to ensure the Armenian character of the autonomy and its preservation. Additional state financing for the Armenian schools in Nagorno-Karabakh can be a positive measure to ensure the quality of education in the autonomy. Moreover, a form of the "regional citizenship", as described earlier, should be allowed and implemented by Azerbaijan to provide the autonomy with important guarantees for the Armenian minority. Additionally, the introduction of Armenian language as a second official state language in Azerbaijan will be a positive step, based on the experience of Finland in this matter. The Armenian minority should be considered an integral part of the people of Azerbaijan and a valued part of the society to be preserved and developed on a par with the rest of its population.

Conclusion

The Nagorno-Karabakh Conflict remains unresolved and somewhat obscure for media coverage and for scholarly attention. Yet this conflict is one of the main threats to the peace and security in a very geopolitically tense region of South Caucasus. The conflict itself has been there for three full decades with no end in sight. More than a quarter of a century of negotiations and attempts to resolve the matter through political means have led to almost no real results. At the same time, the research covering the legal issues of this conflict and public international law stance have also been very scarce and rarely comprehensive.

This book made an attempt to provide a more clear and comprehensive analysis of the issues of international law relevant to the Nagorno-Karabakh Conflict through a comparative legal analysis with the prominent case of the Aland Islands. Moreover, it made an effort to answer the question of whether the Aland Islands precedent can be used as a model for the resolution of the Nagorno-Karabakh Conflict.

The legal analysis conducted in this book clearly shows that in the case of the Nagorno-Karabakh there remains a fact of the occupation of the territory of Azerbaijan by Armenia. In 2015 this fact was reaffirmed by the decision of the ECHR in *Chiragov v. Armenia* case, where the court confirmed the effective control that Armenia has exercised over the territory of the conflict as well as the military presence of Armenia in the territories in question, making the fact of occupation clear. Moreover, the study examined the principle of self-determination in relation to the Nagorno-Karabakh and its population and found that this principle of international law is not applicable in this case in a broader sense (external self-determination), as the Armenian population of Nagorno-Karabakh cannot be considered "people" in the meaning provided by the UN Charter and other relevant treaties. However, as the Armenian population constitutes a minority in Azerbaijan, internal self-determination, in this case, is applicable. The analysis also showed that Nagorno-Karabakh was not able to use USSR's

DOI: 10.4324/9780429353437-5

legislation to complete the process of secession from Azerbaijan, and the region itself does not constitute a *de facto* state, as sometimes argued.

In the case of the Aland Islands precedent, which constitutes a territorial conflict between Sweden and Finland, resolved through an autonomous solution at the beginning of the 20th century, it was possible to discern the key elements of the case that are important from the point of view of public international law. Those elements consist of a very long-lasting demilitarization and neutralization regime of the islands, a very high level of autonomous self-governance and unique standards of minority rights protection. The longevity of the autonomous solution of Aland Islands was also examined as a clear indicator of its success.

Both cases have a unique history and still possess a number of common features in historical retrospective as well as in the issues raised in the conflict from the point of view of international law. Historically, both the Aland Islands and Nagorno-Karabakh were part of Imperial Russia for almost a century before the revolution of 1917. However, the Aland Islands question was resolved shortly after, while the Nagorno-Karabakh issue was somewhat conserved by the policies of the Soviet Union and reemerged at the fall of the USSR. Both conflicts feature a territorial dispute that concerns an area populated by the minority from the neighboring kin-state. Thus, the international legal protection of minorities is applicable to both cases. The same is true for the exercise of internal self-determination that was one of the cornerstones of the resolution of the conflict in Aland Islands. The analyses have also revealed another interesting feature common to both cases – the involvement and high interests of third parties and international organizations. In the case of the Aland Islands, the attention of such states as France and the UK and concerns of other states of the Baltic Sea region were actually helpful for the resolution of the conflict through the League of Nations. In the case of Nagorno-Karabakh, the situation seems to be the opposite. Regional states and extra-regional actors have basically put the conflict into political deadlock. A change in their position towards an international legal solution, following the example of the League of Nations, would be very beneficial for the resolution of the Nagorno-Karabakh Conflict.

Considering the above, the use of the Aland Islands precedent as a model for the resolution of the Nagorno-Karabakh Conflict seems both logical and relevant. However, the "model" here should not mean a simple template application of the features of Aland Islands autonomous solution to the resolution of the Nagorno-Karabakh Conflict. Rather, the best practices of the main elements of the Aland Islands solution can be tailored and applied to the Nagorno-Karabakh Conflict's relevant issues. In the case of security concerns of Armenia for its minority living on the territory of

Nagorno-Karabakh, the demilitarization and neutralization regime (using the example of Aland Islands) can be applied after the end of Armenian occupation, to guarantee the security of the minority population there. Neither Armenia, Azerbaijan or any other state will be able to militarize the region afterward. Moreover, the highest level of self-governance should be guaranteed to Nagorno-Karabakh and the limits and changes of this status will depend on the consent of the authorities of Nagorno-Karabakh. The Aland Islands' mechanisms that provide the constant communication between the state and the autonomy (such as Governor and Delegation of Aland) and effectively serve for the resolution of conflicting situations and delimitation of central and autonomous powers on the regular basis, should also be replicated in some form in Nagorno-Karabakh. The Aland Islands' experience should be used to establish the highest levels of minority rights protection for the Armenian population of Nagorno-Karabakh, as well. The protection of the Armenian minority will play a major role in the resolution of the conflict based on international law. Cultural, linguistic and religious rights of Armenians must be protected.

While attempts to find a political solution are proving to be ineffective, perhaps it is time to consider the implementation and enforcement of international law as an alternative. The transfer of the matter back to the UN from OSCE and establishment of an *ad hoc* body charged with a mandate to find a solution based on international law may be the answer to the Nagorno-Karabakh question. As the results of this book show, the Aland Islands precedent can be used as a model or inspiration for the resolution of the Nagorno-Karabakh Conflict. While Azerbaijan has before signaled that it is ready for an autonomous solution,[249] perhaps Armenia and third states involved in the settlement will follow suit for the establishment of peace and security in the South Caucasus.

249 Euronews, *Ilham Aliyev gave an Interview to "Euronews" TV Channel in Brussels*, 22 June 2011, https://en.president.az/articles/2500.

Bibliography

Ali Abasov and Haroutiun Khachatrian, *The Karabakh Conflict, Variants of Settlement: Concepts and Reality*, Baku/Yerevan: Areat, Noyan Tapan, 2006, http://bit.ly/QWrlTT

Christer Ahlström, 'Demilitarised and Neutralised Zones in a European Perspective', in Lauri Hannikainen and Frank Horn (eds.), *Autonomy and Demilitarisation in International Law: The Åland Islands in a Changing Europe*, Kluwer Law International, 2007.

Sia Spiliopoulou Åkermark, 'Ålands Demilitarisation and Neutralisation: Continuity and Change', in Sia Spiliopoulou Åkermark (ed.), *The Åland Example and Its Components – Relevance for International Conflict Resolution*, Mariehamn: Åland Islands Peace Institute, 2011a.

Sia Spiliopoulou Åkermark, 'Introduction', in Sia Spiliopoulou Åkermark (ed.), *The Åland Example and Its Components – Relevance for International Conflict Resolution*, Mariehamn: Åland Islands Peace Institute, 2011b.

Audrey L. Altstadt, *The Azerbaijani Turks: Power and Identity Under Russian Rule*, Stanford, California: Hoover Institution Press, 1992.

James Barros, *The Aland Islands Question: Its Settlement by the League of the Nations*, New Haven, Connecticut and London: Yale University Press, 1968.

Agha Bayramov, 'Silencing the Nagorno-Karabakh Conflict and Challenges of Four-Day War', *Security and Human Rights*, Volume 27, 2016, pp. 116–127.

C. W. Blandy, Azerbaijan: *Is War Over Nagornyy Karabakh a Realistic Option?*, Advanced Research and Assessment Group, Caucasus Series, 08/17, Defence Academy of the United Kingdom, May 2008, https://www.files.ethz.ch/isn/87342/08_may.pdf

Nina Caspersen, 'Between Puppets and Independent Actors: Kin-state Involvement in the Conflicts in Bosnia, Croatia and Nagorno Karabakh', *Ethnopolitics*, Volume 7, No. 4, November 2008.

Joshua Castellino, 'International Law and Self-Determination. Peoples, Indigenous Peoples and Minorities', in Christian Walter, Antje Von Ungern-Sternberg and Kavus Abushov (eds.), *Self-Determination and Secession in International Law*, Oxford University Press, 2014.

Svante E. Cornell, *The Nagorno-Karabakh Conflict*, Report No. 46, Department of East European Studies, Uppsala University, 1999.

Alexandru-Vlad Crisan, 'The Nagorno-Karabakh Conflict: The Principle of Sovereignty and the Right to Self-Determination', *International Journal of Humanistic Ideology*, Volume 6, Issue 2, Autumn/Winter 2015.

Thomas De Waal, *Black Garden: Armenia and Azerbaijan Through Peace and War*, New York: New York University Press, 2003.

Yoram Dinstein, War, *Aggression and Self-Defence*, 5th ed., New York: Cambridge University Press, 2011.

Matts Dreijer, *The History of the Åland People I:1 From the Stone Age to Gustavus Wasa*, Mariehamn, 1986, p. 561.

Malvina Halberstam, 'The Right to Self-Defense Once the Security Council Takes Action', *Michigan Journal of International Law*, Volume 17, 1996, pp. 229–248.

Lauri Hannikainen, *Cultural Linguistic and Educational Rights in the Åland Islands. An Analysis in International Law*, Helsinki: Publications of the Advisory Board for International Human Rights Affairs No. 5, 1992.

Lauri Hannikainen, 'The International Legal Basis of the Autonomy and Swedish Character of the Åland Islands', in Lauri Hannikainen and Frank Horn (eds.), *Autonomy and Demilitarisation in International Law: The Åland Islands in a Changing Europe*, Kluwer Law International, 2007.

Hurst Hannum, *Documents on Autonomy and Minority Rights*, Dordrecht: Martinus Nijhoff, 1993.

Frank Horn, 'Minorities in Åland with Special Reference to their Educational Rights', in Lauri Hannikainen and Frank Horn (eds.), *Autonomy and Demilitarisation in International Law: The Åland Islands in a Changing Europe*, Kluwer Law International, 2007.

Christer Janson, 'The Autonomy of Aland: A Reflection of International and Constitutional Law', *Nordisk Tidsskrift International Ret*, Volume 51, 1982, pp. 15–22.

Gunnar Jansson, 'Introduction', in Lauri Hannikainen and Frank Horn (eds.), *Autonomy and Demilitarisation in International Law: The Åland Islands in a Changing Europe*, Kluwer Law International, 2007.

Pertti Joenniemi, 'The Åland Islands Issue', in Clive Archer and Pertti Joenniemi (eds.), *The Nordic Peace*, Ashgate, 2003.

Pertti Joenniemi, 'Åland in the New Europe: A Case of Post-Sovereign Political Life', in Lauri Hannikainen and Frank Horn (eds.), *Autonomy and Demilitarisation in International Law: The Åland Islands in a Changing Europe*, Kluwer Law International, 2007.

Kamer Kasim, 'The Nagorno-Karabakh Conflict: Regional Implications and the Peace Process', *Caucasus International* (Ankara: Moda Ofset Basim Yayin), Volume 2, No.1, 2012, pp. 93–110.

Marcelo G. Kohen, 'Introduction' in Marcelo G. Kohen (ed.), *Secession: International Law Perspectives*, New York: Cambridge University Press, 2006.

Heiko Krüger, *The Nagorno-Karabakh Conflict: A Legal Analysis*, London and New York: Springer, 2010.

Heiko Krüger, 'Nagorno-Karabakh', in Christian Walter, Antje Von Ungern-Sternberg and Kavus Abushov (eds.), *Self-Determination and Secession in International Law*, Oxford University Press, 2014.

Ömer E. Lütem, 'Facts and Comments', *Ermeni Araştırmaları/Armenian Studies* (Ankara: ASAM), No. 2, 2001.

Kamal Makili-Aliyev, 'Azerbaijan's Foreign Policy: Between East and West...', *IAI Working Papers*, Rome, Italy, No.1305, 2013a, http://www.iai.it/content.asp?langid=2&contentid=834

Kamal Makili-Aliyev, *Nagorno-Karabakh Conflict in International Legal Documents and International Law*, Baku, SAM, 2013b, http://bit.ly/31qCYY4

Kamal Makili-Aliyev, *Nagorno-Karabakh Isn't Disputed Territory—It's Occupied* – The National Interest (U.S.), May 2016, http://bit.ly/2eQt8v9

Farhad Mehdiyev, Irada Bagirova, Gulshan Pashayeva and Kamal Makili-Aliyev, 'Legal status of Quasi-Autonomies in USSR: Case of Nagorno-Karabakh's Autonomous Oblast', *Caucasus International* (Ankara: Pasifik Ofset Ltd.), Volume 3, No. 1–2, 2013, http://www.academia.edu/5474212/NK_Legal_Status-CI_Vol_3_no_1-2

Carol Migdalovitz, *Armenia-Azerbaijan Conflict*, CRS Issue Brief for Congress, Air University, 8 August 2003, http://www.au.af.mil/au/awc/awcgate/crs/ib92109.pdf

Nicholas W. Miller, 'Nagorno-Karabakh: A War without Peace', in Kristen Eichensehr and W. Michael Reisman (eds.), *Stopping Wars and Making Peace: Studies in International Intervention*, Martin Nijhoff Publishers, 2009.

Elisabeth Naucler, 'The Åland Solution Applied', in Sia Spiliopoulou Åkermark (ed.), *The Åland Example and Its Components – Relevance for International Conflict Resolution*, Mariehamn: Åland Islands Peace Institute, 2011.

Heidi Öst, 'The Cultural and Linguistic Safeguards of the Åland Minority Protection Regime', in Sia Spiliopoulou Åkermark (ed.), *The Åland Example and Its Components – Relevance for International Conflict Resolution*, Mariehamn: Åland Islands Peace Institute, 2011a.

Heidi Öst, 'Åland and the Nagorno-Karabakh Negotiations in the South Caucasus', in Sia Spiliopoulou Åkermark (ed.), *The Åland Example and Its Components – Relevance for International Conflict Resolution*, Mariehamn: Åland Islands Peace Institute, 2011b.

Sten Palmgren, 'The Autonomy of the Åland Islands in the Constitutional Law of Finland', in Lauri Hannikainen and Frank Horn (eds.), *Autonomy and Demilitarisation in International Law: The Åland Islands in a Changing Europe*, Kluwer Law International, 2007.

Anne Peters, 'The Principle of Uti Possidetis Juris. How Relevant is it for Issues of Secession?', in Christian Walter, Antje Von Ungern-Sternberg and Kavus Abushov (eds.), *Self-Determination and Secession in International Law*, Oxford University Press, 2014.

Danny Pieters, *Functions of Comparative Law and Practical Methodology of Comparing. Or How the Goal Determines the Road!*, in Syllabus Research Master in Law, Leuven-Tilburg, 2009, http://bit.ly/2k5e9iI

Thomas K. Plofchan, Jr., 'Article 51: Limits on Self-Defense', *Michigan Journal of International Law*, Volume13, No. 2, 1992, pp. 336–373.

Michla Pomerance, *Self-Determination in Law and Practice: The New Doctrine in* the United Nations, The Hague and London: Martin Nijhoff, 1982.

Tim Potier, *Conflict in Nagorno-Karabakh, Abkhazia and South Ossetia. A Legal Appraisal*, The Hague: Kluwer Law International, 2001.

Shafa Qasimova, 'Article 51 of the UN Charter and the Armenia-Azerbaijan Conflict', *Perceptions*, Spring-Summer 2010, pp. 75–98.

Allan Rosas, 'Åland Islands as a Demilitarised and Neutralised Zone', in Lauri Hannikainen and Frank Horn (eds.), *Autonomy and Demilitarisation in International Law: The Åland Islands in a Changing Europe*, Kluwer Law International, 2007.

Christopher Rossi, 'Nagorno-Karabakh and the Minsk Group: The Imperfect Appeal of Soft Law in an Overlapping Neighborhood', *Texas International Law Journal*, Volume 52, No. 1, 2017, pp. 45–70.

Arsène Saparov, 'Why Autonomy? The Making of Nagorno-Karabakh Autonomous Region 1918–1925', *Europe-Asia Studies*, Volume 64, March 2012, pp. 281–323.

Dinah Shelton, 'Subsidiary, Democracy and Human Rights', in D. Gomien (ed.), *Broadening the Frontiers of Human Rights*, Oslo: Scandinavian University Press, 1993.

William R. Slomanson, 'Nagorno Karabakh: An Alternative Legal Approach to Its Quest for Legitimacy', *Thomas Jefferson Law Review*, Volume 35, No.1, 2012, p. 29.

Sarah Stephan, 'The Autonomy of Åland Islands', in Sia Spiliopoulou Åkermark (ed.), *The Åland Example and Its Components – Relevance for International Conflict Resolution*, Mariehamn: Åland Islands Peace Institute, 2011.

Markku Suksi, 'Explaining the Robustness and Longevity of the Åland Example in Comparison with Other Autonomy Solutions', *International Journal on Minority and Group Rights*, Volume 20, No.1, 2013a, pp. 51–66.

Markku Suksi, 'Prosperity and Happiness Through Autonomy. The Self-Government of the Åland Islands in Finland', in Yash Ghai and Sophia Woodman (eds.), *Practicing Self-Government: A Comparative Study of Autonomous Regions*, Cambridge University Press, 2013b.

Ron Synovitz, 'Open Secret': *Experts Cast Doubt On Yerevan's Claims Over Nagorno-Karabakh*, RFE/RL, 5 April 2016, https://www.rferl.org/a/armenia-nagorno-karabakh-army-synergy/27656532.html

Patrick Thornberry, 'The Principle of Self-Determination', in Vaughan Lowe and Colin Warbrick (eds.), *The United Nations and the Principles of International Law: Essays in Memory of Michael Akehurst*, New York: Routledge, 2002.

Unto Vesa, 'The Åland Islands as a Conflict Resolution Model', in Unto Vesa and Chinsoo Bae (eds.) *Territorial Issues in Europe and East Asia: Colonialism, War Occupation, and Conflict Resolution*, Northeast Asian Foundation, 2009.

Rüdiger Wolfrum, *Max Planck Encyclopedia of Public International Law*, International Law, 2006, http://bit.ly/2kpzSCa

Christopher Zurcher, *Post-Soviet Wars, Rebellion, Ethnic Conflict, and Nationhood in the Caucasus*, New York: New York University Press, 2007.

Primary Sources

1975 Helsinki Final Act.

Act on the Autonomy of Åland (1991/1144), http://www.finlex.fi/en/laki/kaannokset/1991/en19911144.pdf

Case "Relating to Certain Aspects of the Laws on the Use of Languages in Education in Belgium" v. Belgium, No. 1474/62; 1677/62; 1691/62; 1769/63; 1994/63; 2126/64, 1968, http://hudoc.echr.coe.int/eng?i=001-57525

Chiragov and Others v. Armenia [GC], No. 13216/05, ECHR 2015, http://hudoc.echr.coe.int/eng?i=001-155353

CERD General Recommendation XXI (Right to Self-determination), 23 August 1996.

CCPR General Comment No. 12: Article 1 (*Right to Self-determination*), The Right to Self-determination of Peoples, 13 March 1984, http://www.refworld.org/docid/453883f822.html

CCPR General Comment No. 23: Article 27 *(Rights of Minorities)*, 8 April 1994, CCPR/C/21/Rev.1/Add.5, http://www.refworld.org/docid/453883fc0.html

Constitution of Azerbaijan, 1995, http://en.president.az/azerbaijan/constitution

Council of Europe, *European Charter for Regional or Minority Languages*, 5 November 1992, ETS 148, http://www.coe.int/en/web/conventions/full-list/-/conventions/rms/0900001680695175

Council of Europe, *European Convention for the Protection of Human Rights and Fundamental Freedoms, as amended by Protocols Nos. 11 and 14*, 4 November 1950, ETS 5, http://www.echr.coe.int/Documents/Convention_ENG.pdf

European Parliament Resolution of 20 May 2010 on the Need for an EU Strategy for the South Caucasus (2009/2216(INI)).

OIC Resolution No. 10/11-P(IS) on the Aggression of the Republic of Armenia against the Republic of Azerbaijan. https://en.wikipedia.org/wiki/OIC_Resolution_10/11

Human Rights Watch/Helsinki, Azerbaijan. *Seven Years of Conflict in Nagorno-Karabakh*, 8 December 1994, http://bit.ly/2w3R9q7

International Crisis Group, *Nagorno-Karabakh: Risking War*, Europe Report No. 187, I n.2, 2007.

International Law Commission, *The Report of the International Law Commission*, 53rd Session, GAOR, 56th Session, Supp. No.10 (A/56/10), 2001.

Joint Statement on the Nagorno-Karabakh Conflict by U.S. President Obama, Russian President Medvedev, and French President Sarkozy at the L'Aquila Summit of the Eight, 10 July 2009, http://1.usa.gov/1ioVvX6

Lisbon Document 1996, OSCE Lisbon Summit 1996, http://www.osce.org/mc/39539?download=true

Muradyan v. Armenia [GC], No. 11275/07, ECHR 2016, http://hudoc.echr.coe.int/eng?i=001-168852

NATO, *Chicago Summit Declaration.*

OHCHR, *Minority Rights: International Standards and Guidance for Implementation*, UN, 2010, http://www.ohchr.org/Documents/Publications/MinorityRights_en.pdf

PACE Resolution 1416 (2005) "The Conflict over the Nagorno-Karabakh Region Dealt with by the OSCE Minsk Conference".

Rome Statute of the International Criminal Court, 1998, http://bit.ly/1TeuDLN

Statistics Finland, *Finland in Figures 2019*, Helsinki: Grano Oy, 2019, http://bit.ly/2K2ggyV

The World Factbook 2017. Washington, DC: Central Intelligence Agency, 2017.

The Åland Agreement in the Council of the League of Nations, Minutes of the Seventeenth Meeting of the Council, June 27th, *League of Nations Official Journal*, September 1921.

UN Charter, 1945, http://www.un.org/en/charter-united-nations/index.html

UN General Assembly, *Agenda for Peace*, A/47/277, S/24111, 1992, http://www.un-documents.net/a47-277.htm

UN General Assembly, *Convention on the Rights of the Child*, A/RES/44/25, 1989, http://www.ohchr.org/EN/ProfessionalInterest/Pages/CRC.aspx

UN General Assembly, *Declaration on the Granting of Independence to Colonial Countries and Peoples*, 1960, A/RES/15/1514, http://www.un.org/en/decolonization/declaration.shtml

UN General Assembly, *Declaration on Principles of International Law Concerning Friendly Relations and Co-Operation among States in Accordance with the Charter of the United Nations*, 1970, A/RES/25/2625, http://www.un-documents.net/a25r2625.htm

UN General Assembly, *Resolution 3314 (XXIX).*

UN General Assembly, *Resolution 62/243.*

UN General Assembly, *Declaration on the Rights of Persons belonging to the National or Ethnic, Religious and Linguistic Minorities*, 1992, A/RES/47/135

UN General Assembly, *International Covenant on Civil and Political Rights*, General Assembly resolution 2200A (XXI), 1966, http://bit.ly/1Oq5JFt

UN General Assembly, *International Covenant on Economic, Social and Cultural Rights*, General Assembly resolution 2200A (XXI), 1966, http://bit.ly/J1E1V3

UNESCO, *Convention against Discrimination in Education*, 14 December 1960, http://www.unesco.org/education/pdf/DISCRI_E.PDF

World Bank Data, *Azerbaijan*, 2018, https://data.worldbank.org/country/azerbaijan

Декларация Азербайджанской Республики, Республики Армения и Российской Федерации, 2 ноября 2008 года, Московская область, http://archive.kremlin.ru/text/docs/2008/11/208670.shtml

Index